THE
MARKETING
PLAN

THE PROFESSIONAL PAPERBACK SERIES

The *Professional Paperback Series*, new from Kogan Page, is a major series of practically focused business books aimed at professionals in the middle to senior management bracket. The series covers a wide range of leading edge business topics, including business strategy, organizational theory and design, leadership, marketing, project management and management style. This invaluable series is a mixture of new titles and new or revised editions of best-selling titles. For both practising managers and students of business, the *Professional Paperback Series* will give a boost to their skills and knowledge.

Titles currently available in the series are:

Commonsense Direct Marketing
Fourth edition
Drayton Bird

Transform Your Management Style!
How to Develop and Motivate Your Staff to Achieve Peak Performance
Hilary Walmsley

Total Leadership
How to Inspire and Motivate Through Effective Leadership
Jim Barrett

Designing Organizations
The Foundation for Excellence
Third edition
Philip Sadler

The Top Consultant
Developing Your Skills for Greater Effectiveness
Third edition
Calvert Markham

The Marketing Plan
A Practitioner's Guide
Second edition
John Westwood

Goal Directed Project Management
Second edition
E S Andersen, K V Grude and T Haug

Creating a World Class Organization
Ten Performance Measures of Business Success
Second edition
Bryan D Prescott

PROFESSIONAL
PAPERBACKS

THE
MARKETING
PLAN

A Practitioner's Guide
Second Edition

John Westwood

INSTITUTE OF DIRECTORS

**KOGAN
PAGE**

LONDON, UK • NEW HAMPSHIRE, USA • NEW DELHI, INDIA

<u>YOURS TO HAVE AND TO HOLD</u>
BUT NOT TO COPY

First published in 1990
Second edition published in 1996
Reprinted as part of the Professional Paperbacks series in 1998
Reprinted 1998

Kogan Page Limited
120 Pentonville Road
London
N1 9JN

Kogan Page Limited
163 Central Avenue, Suite 4
Dover, NH 03820
USA

The Institute of Directors accepts no responsibility for the opinions expressed by the author of this publication. Readers should consult their advisors before acting on any of the issues raised.

British Library Cataloguing in Publication Data
A CIP record for this book is available from the British Library.
ISBN 0 7494 2614 4

Typeset by Palimpsest Book Production Limited, Polmont, Stirlingshire
Printed in England by Clays Ltd, St Ives plc

Contents

Introduction

No company can survive in the modern world unless it plans for the future. Marketing planning is the technique that enables a company to decide on the best use of its scarce resources to achieve its corporate objectives. The marketing plan is the passport to this future.

This book is a step-by-step practical guide to the marketing planning process and to the preparation of all types of marketing plans. Whether the intention is to prepare a full marketing plan for the company or a specific marketing plan for an individual product or market, it can be achieved by following the procedures detailed here.

It explains in simple language exactly what a marketing plan is and why *every* company needs one. The fundamentals of marketing planning are outlined and the basic structures of different types of marketing plan are detailed. The reader is then gradually taken through the various steps involved in putting together a marketing plan.

Sources of market information, both within and outside the company, are examined. Sample forms, questionnaires and document layouts are included. Methods of collecting, analysing and presenting information are explained.

The planning process involves a full analysis of the strengths and weaknesses of the company, its organization and its products.

Guidelines are given for the setting of achievable marketing objectives, and methods of determining marketing strategies to reach these objectives are explained. The action plans are the all-important programmes for carrying out the strategies.

The different approaches necessary for different areas and applications are explained: capital goods contrast with consumer goods and services; the new product is particularly difficult because it has no history and no track record. Guidance is given on the different approaches necessary in different markets such as Europe, North America and the Far East.

The budgeting process is explained and the costs of implementing a plan are compared with the return to the company if the plan is successful.

Finally, guidance is given on how the written plan should be put together, presented and implemented.

The Marketing Plan is aimed at the sales and marketing professional at any stage in his or her career. It is intended to take the mystery and mystique out of preparing marketing plans. It is a practical workbook enabling all marketeers to grasp the fundamentals of marketing planning and to prepare professional marketing plans themselves.

1: What is a Marketing Plan and Why Do You Need One?

A company's management has many important roles. It sets objectives, and develops plans, policies, procedures, strategies and tactics. It organizes and co-ordinates, directs and controls, motivates and communicates. Planning is only one of its roles but it is an important one: the company's corporate or business plan runs the business.

The marketing plan is one part, albeit an important part, of this plan. The marketing planning process therefore needs to be carried out as part of the overall company planning and budgeting process.

There are a number of different approaches that a company can adopt in planning for the future. In traditional planning, the plans can be differentiated according to the time-scales they cover, ie:

• long-term plans

• medium-term plans

• short-term plans

There is no universal definition of the length of time covered by these types of plans. Long- and medium-term plans are often defined as 'strategic' plans because they consider the longer-term strategies for the business, and short-term plans are often defined as 'corporate' or 'business' plans because they are plans that 'run' the business on a day-to-day basis. The use of these plans depends on the type of business the company is in, the markets that it serves and the need for future planning of products and expansion.

Long-term planning aims to assess future economic and business trends for many years ahead. It enables a company to determine strategies that will sustain growth and meet corporate objectives in the long-term. It is of particular importance in areas such as defence, aerospace and for pharmaceutical products where the development times for new products may be as long as five or ten years. Long-term planning in these cases may cover periods of up to ten or twenty years. Most companies do not, however, have such long product development times and in these companies long-term planning looks no further ahead than five or seven years.

Medium-term planning is more practical and normally covers a period of two to five years (with three years being the most common). This is a more practical exercise because the planners are nearer to the present. Fewer assumptions need to be made and the plan is more likely to reflect what will actually happen. The medium-term 'strategic' plan will reflect the strategies developed in the long-term plan, but it will include the major decisions necessary in the shorter term. These decisions will include such things as the introduction of new products, capital investment requirements, and the availability and utilization of personnel and resources.

Short-term planning (and budgeting) normally covers a one-year period and produces the company 'corporate' or 'business' plan with its associated budgets. This is a plan that covers the immediate future and details what the company intends to do over a twelve-month period (tied in to the company's financial year). Short-term plans are produced in much more detail than other types of plans. They may also be revised within the year if necessary.

Traditional planning and strategic planning

Before the 1970s traditional strategic and corporate planning worked well. Business cycles were fairly predictable, the environment was stable, competitors were well known, major exchange rates were fixed, industry pricing was stable and customers behaved in a predictable way.

Since the oil shocks of the 1970s and the move to floating exchange rates, companies have been faced with a radically different and rapidly changing environment. New technology, new competition, large changes in costs and other, irreversible changes, demanded a different type of strategic planning process. This involved formulating a view of the business and its competitive environment in the future, and deciding the immediate steps that must be achieved in the short term. So the focus shifted from long-term planning to the implementation of action plans which would produce visible short-term results and against the results of which the long-term strategic plan could be further refined. The planning horizon was reduced to no more than a few years.

The fundamental difference between the two approaches is that in traditional planning it is assumed that all relevant information is available at the beginning of the process, whereas the new 'strategic' planning approach is designed to react to and exploit new information as it is acquired. The 'strategic' planning approach is the approach now adopted by marketing planners.

What is the difference between a marketing plan and a company's corporate plan?

The directors and senior management of a company set its corporate objectives. These are normally expressed in financial terms and will define what the company aims to be at some time in the future – say three years' time. The corporate objectives will include such things as sales turnover, profit before tax, return on capital, etc. To produce a workable corporate plan, a company must first gather information about its current operations. This is called an audit. Each function in the company will carry out its own audit. The audits will suggest certain objectives and strategies. This will result in a plan for each functional area of the company for achieving its individual set of objectives and for implementing its particular strategies. The individual plans will include figures for the approximate costs and revenues and will be worked out in detail for the first year of the plan.

The marketing plan sets out the marketing objectives of the company and suggests strategies for achieving these objectives. It does not include all of the corporate objectives and strategies of the company. There will also be production objectives, financial objectives, and personnel objectives. None of these objectives can be set in isolation.

The full corporate or business plan for the company will include a number of sub-plans *including* the overall company marketing plan. All of the individual plans need to be agreed and co-ordinated into the one corporate plan. The structure of the corporate plan is shown in Figure 1.1.

In this book we will be specifically concerned with just one part of the corporate plan – the marketing plan – but we need to consider the difficulties encountered in producing objectives and strategies within the whole organization.

The order intake and sales budgets which will be part of the marketing plan will drive the corporate plan. None of the other plans can be completed without this information. It will determine the sales output for the production plan, with implications also for purchasing, stock levels, and stock turnover. This in turn will affect invoicing, cash flow, and the funding of trade credit in the finance plan.

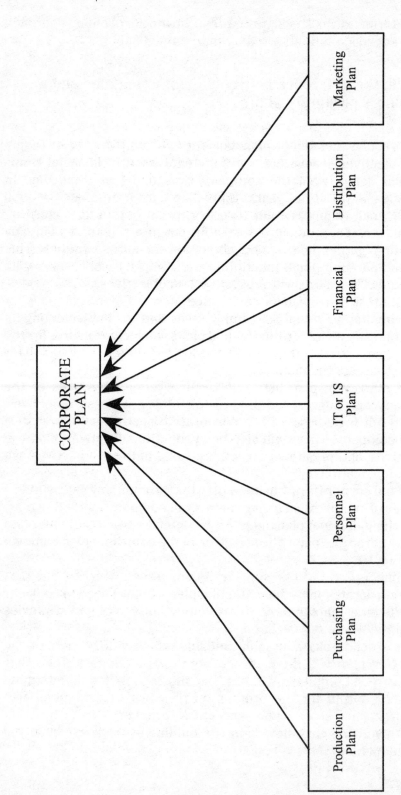

Figure 1.1 The structure of a company corporate plan

There are also other issues which, if included in the marketing plan, would have implications on the other plans. Pricing issues would affect the finance plan, and the marketing plan will recommend pricing policies and strategies. The introduction of a new product would have major implications for the production plan. It might also involve the financing of strategic stocks. Stocks might also be supplied on a consignment basis to help penetrate new strategic markets. Decisions would be taken in the production and purchasing plans on whether to manufacture certain components 'in house' or to buy them in from outside. If the marketing plan was for a replacement or enhanced product and price was a key factor in its success, it might be that it was cheaper to have the product 'made out' by another manufacturer. What would be the opportunity cost to production (and its plan) of the surplus production capacity and what would be the implications for the finance plan of funding the 'buying out' and the carrying of stocks if the purchasing of economic batches was appropriate?

All of these factors (and many others) need to be discussed and negotiated with other functional heads and with top management early in the marketing planning process as they lay down basic parameters for the marketing planner.

A marketing plan is like a map – it shows a company where it is going and how it is going to get there. It is both an action plan and a written document. A marketing plan should identify the most promising business opportunities for the company and outline how to penetrate, capture and maintain positions in identified markets. It is a communication tool combining all the elements of the marketing mix into a co-ordinated action plan. It spells out who will do what, when, where and how, to achieve its ends.

Most other books on marketing planning concentrate on theory. This approach is fine for business academics but makes the whole process too complicated for the average sales manager. My approach is a practical one, including only as much theory as is necessary to understand the planning process. From a personal point of view, I believe that you will find that adopting and following the formal structure of a plan as laid down in this book will make it easier to order your thoughts and the facts logically.

It will be easier:

- For the people reading the plan to follow your arguments and to see how you reached your conclusions.

- For you to present a professional-looking and complete document from even a relatively small amount of information.

What is marketing and how does it differ from selling?

Successful marketing involves having the *right* product available in the *right* place at the *right* time and making sure that the customer is aware of the product.

Selling is a straightforward concept which involves persuading a customer to buy a product. It is, however, only one aspect of the marketing process.

Most people in sales will have been on one or more sales training courses. These courses will be selling-orientated, of the type run by the Institute of Sales Engineers or the many private courses run by a wide variety of training organizations. As well as general courses that individual sales people can attend, there are also many organizations now that run excellent in-house sales training courses that are tailor-made for a particular company. They are good at teaching the basics about selling and selling situations and cover everything from the obvious to the more important techniques of closing the sale. But they teach you virtually nothing about marketing, because that is not their function.

Even now, in large companies, the sales and marketing functions are often completely separated, sometimes with different directors for 'sales' and for 'marketing'. In some organizations, sales is a local function and marketing is handled in isolation by head office or by a 'marketing executive'. This should not be the case. The sales and marketing functions need to be combined or at least run with the same company aims. There must be a continuous interchange of information between the sales function and the marketing function, otherwise it will have an adverse effect on marketing planning.

The separation of the sales and marketing functions can create difficulties for sales personnel when they need to become involved in marketing and marketing planning. Even now it is possible to find sales directors, particularly in small companies, who have no formal marketing training. With sales managers the situation is worse and sales engineers, even in large companies, are unlikely to have had any training in marketing at all. How then are the sales engineers of today to become the sales managers of tomorrow and the sales and marketing directors of the next decade? Only by learning the tricks of the trade themselves. They can do this in part by learning from others who already have the experience, but formal training is also necessary.

It is taken for granted that large companies, particularly multi-nationals, can afford to train personnel specifically for marketing functions, or can poach experts if they do not already have them in-house. Ten years ago, marketing training was difficult to obtain; that is no longer the case. The same types of organizations that run sales-orientated courses also run marketing courses at various levels. Part-time courses and evening classes are now available from a wide variety of Colleges of Further Education and Universities. Excellent courses are run by the Chartered Institute of Marketing and by the Institute of Sales and Marketing Management. The Open University Business School runs comprehensive courses on marketing and export marketing. These courses have the added advantage of the presence of a tutor.

Sales and marketing personnel will often say that they do not have the time to attend or participate in such courses. However, it may be that the company cannot afford for them not to! Short residential courses are often the answer for more senior personnel. They have the advantage of getting them 'off-site' where they cannot be contacted and where they can concentrate on the course in isolation.

The dictionary definition of marketing is: 'the provision of goods or services to meet consumer needs.' In other words, marketing involves finding out what the customer wants and matching a company's products to meet those requirements, and in the process making a profit for the company. Gone are the days when companies would develop a product and then look for customers for it.

Customers will only buy what they want. Powerful advertising is often criticized as being a tool that allows companies to persuade customers to buy what the company wants to sell. This is just not true – look at Coca Cola's attempt to introduce a new-formula Coca Cola, or the initial reaction to Ford's Sierra.

Two-thirds of new products fail in the marketplace. Companies have to listen to customers and the market and adapt their products accordingly. They have to become 'market-orientated'. A company manufacturing radio sets in the 1950s would have had to change to transistor radios in the 1960s and 1970s and radio/cassette players in the 1980s. A television manufacturer would have made black and white television sets in the 1950s and 1960s, moved into colour television in the 1970s, teletext in the 1980s, and HDTV in the 1990s. Each of these products satisfies the same basic customer desire, but at a different moment in time. If these companies had continued to make only the products that satisfied the customers in the 1960s, they would have gone out of business in the 1970s and 1980s. This is the key fundamental of marketing – 'in the end customers will always get what they want', and the inflexible manufacturer who does not adapt to the market will eventually go out of business.

Marketing is the process that brings together the abilities of a company and the requirements of its customers:

- the customer receives the benefits that satisfy his requirements

- the company receives payment for the goods and makes some profit.

Companies have to be flexible in order to achieve this balance in the marketplace. They must be prepared to change products, introduce new products or enter new markets. They must be able to read their customers and the marketplace. This balancing process takes place in the 'marketing environment'. There are a number of important factors that affect the way the marketing balance is achieved in practice and affect the marketing environment.

Local and cultural preferences

Some customers show a preference for particular products or an aversion to others based on local traditions, local conditions, or for national cultural reasons. British black puddings and shepherd's pie are not likely to sell in large quantities in Italy or Spain and Sauerkraut is unlikely to sell well in Scotland. American refrigerators are too large to fit into Japanese homes.

Government policies

Economic, political, legal or environmental policies in countries where you wish to sell your product can affect what you can do in those countries. Varying exchange rates will affect the viability of your product against locally manufactured products in a particular country and may influence a decision to manufacture locally. Environmental policies may affect car manufacturers and also soap and detergent manufacturers, for example. Government legislation regulates the sale of drugs and pharmaceutical products and certain types of fertilizers and pesticides may be controlled or banned in certain countries.

Competition

What your company does affects your competitors and what your competitors do affects what your company will do and will make. Products, pricing and many other factors are influenced by what the competition does. Even the market leader cannot be complacent and must monitor what his competitors are up to.

New technology

Technology is now changing very fast and customer requirements are changing with it. Digital watches had a profound effect on the watch market. Electric windows and sun-roofs used to be expensive extras on up-market cars; now they are considered standard on top-of-the-range models from all manufacturers. The functions of video recorders are changing all the time. A company cannot assume that its current ranges of products will continue to be in demand for ever. Products have to be modified, improved or replaced as technology advances and changes.

Changing distribution patterns

The advent of hypermarkets and out-of-town shopping centres in the 1970s and 1980s transformed the pattern of the distribution of everything from food to DIY products in Europe. The increase in car ownership facilitated such a change. Japan is in the early stages of such a change and still has much larger numbers of shops per head of population than the USA and Europe. Similarly dramatic changes in distribution patterns have been caused by the introduction of containerization and increased use and availability of air freight.

So, it is clear that the marketing environment in which we operate is not controlled by individuals or companies. It is constantly changing and must be monitored continuously.
   Marketing therefore involves:

• the abilities of the company

• the requirements of the customer

• the marketing environment

The abilities of the company can be managed by the marketing organization. They can control four main elements of a company's operation, which are often referred to as 'the marketing mix'. This relates to:

• the product sold (Product)

• the pricing policy (Price)

• how the product is promoted (Promotion)

• methods of distribution (Place)

'Promotion' and 'Place' are concerned with reaching your potential customers in the first place and 'Products' and 'Price' will allow you to satisfy the customer's requirements.

The 'marketing mix' is often known as the 'four Ps'. They are four controllable variables which allow a company to come up with a policy which is profitable and satisfies its customers.

Markets usually consist of a number of sub-markets with different customer requirements. A company must create an appropriate marketing mix for each of their sub-markets. As an example, the car sales market consists of fleet markets, the company car market, and the private car market – each with its own special requirements.

Each element of the marketing mix is a continuing opportunity to the marketing organization – it must be considered separately and in relation to the other elements of the marketing mix. A mix which is satisfactory at one moment in time may need to be revised because:

• products or services will become obsolete or will be improved

• new products or services will be introduced

• prices may be reduced by the competition and this may reduce margins

• promotion may not be as effective as that of the competition

• the place of sale or method of distribution may become less satisfactory as alternatives arise or the business changes.

Controlling the marketing mix is the key to successful marketing and this is the essence of marketing planning.

What is marketing planning?

The term marketing planning is used to describe the methods of applying marketing resources to achieve marketing objectives. This may sound simple, but it is in fact a very complex process. The resources and the objectives will vary from company to company and will also change with time. Marketing planning is used to segment markets, identify market position, forecast market size, and to plan a viable market share within each market segment.

The process involves:

• Carrying out marketing research within and outside the company

- Looking at the company's strengths and weaknesses
- Making assumptions
- Forecasting
- Setting marketing objectives
- Generating marketing strategies
- Defining programmes
- Setting budgets
- Reviewing the results and revising the objectives, strategies or programmes.

The planning process will:

- Make better use of company resources to identify marketing opportunities
- Encourage team spirit and company identity
- Help the company to move towards achieving its corporate goals

In addition, the marketing research carried out as part of the planning process will provide a solid base of information for present and future projects.

What is a marketing plan?

A marketing plan is a document which formulates a plan for marketing products and services. Although 'products' are referred to in this chapter, the product would nearly always include some 'service' component such as after-sales service, advice by technically trained salespeople, and (with consumer products) in-store merchandizing. A marketing plan has formal structure, but can be used as a formal or informal document which has great flexibility. It can be used to:

- Prepare an argument for introducing a new product
- Revamp the marketing approach for existing products
- Put together a complete departmental, divisional or company marketing plan to be included in the company corporate or business plan

It can refer to a regional, national or worldwide market.

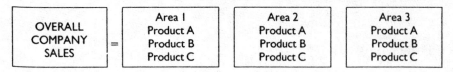

Figure 1.2 Company sales by area

In a centralized company operating out of one base, the split of products and areas can be represented as shown in Figure 1.2. It is therefore possible for such a company to prepare not only an overall marketing plan for all products in all areas, but also to prepare individual plans for individual products or individual sales areas. These are represented in Figures 1.3 and 1.4 respectively.

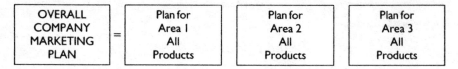

Figure 1.3 Marketing plans prepared by area

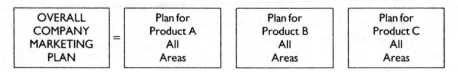

Figure 1.4 Marketing plans prepared by product

In principle it is possible to prepare plans for single products in individual areas. In practice, some individual plans will be prepared, but wider-ranging plans are more common.

As we progress through this book we will frequently look at examples from different industries. These examples will be taken from the consumer and capital goods industries and also from the service industries. In spite of what would appear to be fundamental differences between these types of products, key marketing principles apply equally to the marketing of all of them. The way the principles are applied takes a different form in the consumer, capital, and service sectors. Nevertheless, the fundamental approach to the preparation of a marketing plan is the same.

Figures 1.5, 1.6 and 1.7 show how marketing plans could be prepared in companies in the consumer, capital goods, and service industries. The examples relate to a company manufacturing

TV sets and video recorders (consumer) (Figure 1.5); a company selling capital equipment used in the dairy and brewing industries (capital goods) (Figure 1.6); and an insurance company (service) (Figure 1.7).

OVERALL COMPANY MARKETING PLAN =	Plan for UK TV Sets	Plan for Europe TV Sets	Plan for Rest Of World
	Plan for UK Video Recorders	Plan for Europe Video Recorders	All Products

Figure 1.5 Example of plans for company manufacturing TV sets and video recorders (consumer goods)

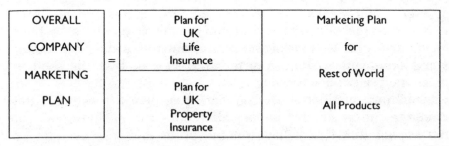

OVERALL COMPANY MARKETING PLAN =	Plan for UK Dairy Industry	Plan for Europe Dairy Industry	Plan for ROW Dairy Industry
	Marketing Plan All Areas Brewing Industry		

Figure 1.6 Example of plans for company manufacturing equipment used in the dairy and brewing industries (capital goods)

OVERALL COMPANY MARKETING PLAN =	Plan for UK Life Insurance	Marketing Plan for Rest of World
	Plan for UK Property Insurance	All Products

Figure 1.7 Example of plans for insurance company (service industry)

Nothing is too small or too large to be covered by a marketing plan. You can write a plan for dairy equipment in Shropshire, diaphragm valves in Belgium, or bathroom suites for hotels in the Middle East. Equally, you can write your plan for your product in the chemical industry or the fast food industry. Even this can be broken down regionally, nationally or internationally.

In a company with a number of subsidiaries, there will be marketing plans in each company whether they are put together by personnel in the subsidiary companies or by head office personnel. Each of these subsidiary marketing plans may be made up of smaller individual marketing plans.

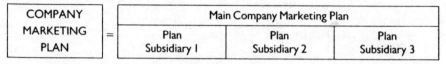

COMPANY MARKETING PLAN =	Main Company Marketing Plan		
	Plan Subsidiary 1	Plan Subsidiary 2	Plan Subsidiary 3

Figure 1.8 Marketing plans of company with subsidiaries

The key factor is that each of the smaller plans should tie in with the overall company plan. It does not mean that you need to prepare a plan for each product or each sales area. Although, if you do prepare an individual marketing plan for a product or an area, that plan must fit in with the overall company marketing plan.

A marketing plan is not complete unless it includes historical data, future predictions, objectives and the methods or strategies to be used to achieve those objectives. If the plan is for a new product there is no historical data relating to that product, but there will be historical data relating to the product that it is superseding, or estimated data relating to equivalent competitors' products in the market.

In its simplest form a marketing plan can start off as a collection and assessment of historical data. It should contain details of competitors including their advantages and disadvantages, strengths and weaknesses. It should also include your own company's strengths and weaknesses, successes and failures. In this form it is not a true plan, but the *start* of a plan. It can then be built on to give a projection for the future, but this projection cannot stand alone without details of the strategies that will be used to make the predictions come true.

In its most compete form the marketing plan will estimate the resources necessary for its execution and will include details of the impact that it will have on the profit and loss account or income statement to be included in the company corporate or business plan.

Why do you and your company need a marketing plan?

Some companies avoid marketing planning because of the time and effort needed to express their policy in written form. Some senior executives think that their time is too valuable to be spent on anything other than pressing day-to-day operational problems. The manager who devotes his time to dealing only with current administrative detail has almost certainly ignored proper planning in the past.

You may think that you do not need a formal marketing plan. Many people survive for the whole of their working lives in sales and marketing without ever writing a marketing plan – or do they?

It is not possible to run a sales organization, however small, or even to prepare a sales forecast, without putting together some rudimentary form of marketing plan. Often, however, figures are put together and then a narrative is prepared to fit in with the figures. This is the wrong way to do it and shows a lack of understanding of the marketing planning process.

In highly competitive times it is necessary to be able to use 'marketing' to channel 'sales' in the right direction. The marketing plan is one of the instruments that enables you to do this. As a document with a formal structure, a marketing plan disciplines the writer to put his thoughts, facts and conclusions down in a logical manner that can be followed by others.

If it is properly prepared, a marketing plan will contain sufficient detail of the company's policies and strategies for its day-to-day implementation to be undertaken by junior management, leaving senior managers free to manage. Only difficult or unusual situations would need to be dealt with by senior management.

Sales personnel at all levels should endeavour to understand marketing and marketing plans. It is important for you, but it is also important for your company. You can be sure that your major competitors will be becoming increasingly professional in their marketing efforts from year to year. Your company needs to be ahead of the competition.

Summary

Planning is one of the most important roles of management. The company's corporate or business plan runs the business. The marketing plan is only one part of the corporate plan and the marketing planning process therefore needs to be carried out as part of the overall company planning and budgeting process.

Because of major changes in the business environment in the 1970s and 1980s, the focus has shifted away from long-term planning to the implementation of action plans which will produce visible short-term results and against the results of which longer-term strategic plans can be further refined. This new 'strategic' planning is designed to react to and exploit new information as it is acquired. This is the approach adopted by marketing planners.

To prepare its corporate plan, a company must set corporate objectives, carry out audits and prepare individual plans for each functional area of the company. All of the plans need to be agreed and co-ordinated into one corporate plan – the marketing plan is one of these plans.

Selling involves persuading the customer to buy your product, but it is only one aspect of the marketing process. Marketing involves finding out what the customer wants and matching your company's products and services to meet these requirements, and in the process making a profit for your company.

This involves understanding:

• the abilities of your company

• the requirements of your customers

• the marketing environment in which you operate

The abilities of the company can be managed by controlling four main elements of a company's operation, often referred to as the marketing mix. These elements are:

• the product sold (Product)

• the pricing policy (Price)

• how the product is promoted (Promotion)

• the methods of distribution (Place)

Marketing planning involves the application of marketing resources to achieve marketing objectives. It is used to segment markets, identify market position, forecast market size and plan a viable market share within each market segment.

Key marketing principles apply equally to the marketing of consumer and capital goods and to services.

A marketing plan is a document which formulates a plan for marketing products and/or services. The overall company marketing plan can be made up of a number of smaller marketing plans for individual products or areas.

A company marketing plan sets out the company's marketing objectives and suggests strategies to achieve them.

2: The Structure of the Plan

It is common to think of a marketing plan as the company marketing plan. There are, however, many types of marketing plan. Not everyone needs or wants to prepare a full-blown company marketing plan. There will be occasions when you want to prepare a plan for a particular product or area. Alternatively, you may want to analyse historical data so that you can understand the potential market for the product or the potential for the product itself. The principles of marketing planning can be equally well applied to a single market or market sector as to the whole of a company's business. You may be at a level in the company where the preparation of a full company marketing plan is not within your brief, but you will still need to be able to prepare marketing plans for your own areas of responsibility.

The requirements will also vary from company to company. A small company may not wish to go into the same detail as a larger company and naturally it will not have the same resources. A short plan, perhaps only a few pages in length, may suffice for a small company whereas, for a larger company, a much longer and more comprehensive document may be necessary.

Regardless of the scope of the plan, or the detail that may be required, the procedure to be adopted and the structure of the final written plan should always be broadly similar.

It is useful when progressing into new areas of activity to be able to put together ground rules and standard formats. Whether this is for standard letters, standard quotations or marketing plans, there is no doubt that it is easier, both for you and for those who will read your documents, to adopt the same basic structure every time.

Stages in the preparation of a marketing plan

Before preparing a marketing plan it is necessary to understand the principles of marketing planning. It is important to detail this planning process as well as considering how to lay out the written document.

The stages in the marketing planning process are shown in Figure 2.1.

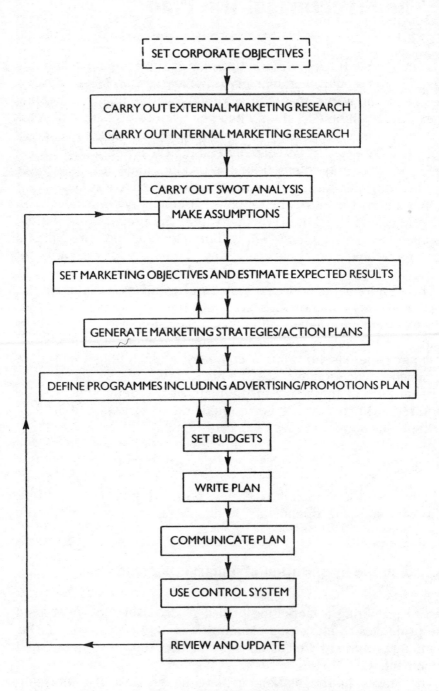

Figure 2.1 The marketing planning process

Set corporate objectives

Corporate objectives are set by top management and this may therefore not be in your brief. Even so, you must be aware of your company's corporate objectives and the ultimate plan should generally be in line with them. Corporate objectives are normally expressed in financial terms and they define what the company aims to be at some time in the future. They will relate to such things as turnover, profit before tax, return on capital, return on investment, etc.

The corporate objective relating to turnover could be 'to increase turnover by 10 per cent per year in real terms over the next 3 years. This is to be achieved by 2 per cent organic growth with 8 per cent by acquisition'. The marketing planner would then know that his plans should show how 2 per cent organic growth is to be achieved. Since it is growth in real terms, it means that if the inflation rate is 5 per cent per annum, a growth rate of 7 per cent per year in terms of turnover must be achieved to give the 2 per cent real growth figure.

Carry out external marketing research

Since companies exist and operate in the marketing environment, the first step in any marketing plan is research into that environment. Research is carried out into the markets themselves and then the information collected is analysed in the context of the marketing of the products. Before looking at in-house data, it is important to collect and analyse external data relating to the markets that the plan will cover. This is key information concerning the companies, industries and countries/areas that the product is being sold in, as well as information on the customers and competitors. This information as such will not ultimately be included in the written plan, but it will be used – particularly in the SWOT analysis.

In addition to information on the marketing environment, information should also be collected on the business and economic environment as they will affect your business. This would include economic factors such as past, present and forecast inflation rates and exchange rates for areas or countries to be covered by the plan. It would also include political, fiscal, environmental, social or cultural factors that could affect your business.

Carry out internal marketing research

Perhaps even more important than general market information is historical information available 'in house'. This will be sales/order and margin/profit data relating specifically to the products and areas for the plan. There will also be other data of a more specific or technical nature. This could include customer industry codes and sales by application or industry sector. This information needs to be put into context in the form of market shares by geographical area and industry type for individual products and in total.

Internal marketing research will also include a detailed study of the company's marketing mix – its products/services, prices, promotion (including advertising, PR and sales promotion) and distribution – as well as looking at the company's marketing organization, before- and after-sales service, marketing research systems, present marketing objectives and strategies, planning and control systems.

Carry out SWOT analysis

When all of the information and opinions have been collected by marketing research, the material needs to be analysed and presented in a way that will help to make the best decisions. This can be done by selecting the key information and carrying out a SWOT analysis.

SWOT analysis stands for:

'Strengths' and 'Weaknesses' as they relate to our 'Opportunities' and 'Threats' in the marketplace.

Strengths and weaknesses relate to the company and its strategies and how it compares with the competition. Opportunities and threats are presented both by the marketing environment and by the competition. SWOT analysis considers company organization, company performance, key products and strategic markets.

If carried out properly, SWOT analysis allows you to focus your attention on the key areas of your business where you have specific knowledge and to make assumptions in areas where your knowledge is lacking. The method of carrying out SWOT analysis is explained in detail in Chapter 5.

Make assumptions

The plan itself has to be based on a clearly understood set of assumptions. These relate to external economic factors as well as technological and competitive factors. Assumptions could relate to inflation rates, currency exchange rates or market growth rates. They could relate to the effect of price competition on price levels in the industry. They should be few in number and should relate only to key issues. If the plan could be implemented regardless of an assumption, that assumption is not necessary and should be removed from the plan.

Set marketing objectives and estimate expected results

The next step is the key to the whole marketing process: the setting of marketing objectives. This is what you want to achieve – the fundamental aims of the plan. A marketing objective concerns the balance between products and their markets. It relates to *which products* you want to sell into *which markets*. It is important not to confuse objectives with strategies. An objective is what you want to achieve; a strategy is how you get there. Objectives will therefore include such things as the anticipated order intake, the sales turnover, market shares and profit levels. The setting of objectives is covered in Chapter 6.

Generate marketing strategies and action plans

Marketing strategies are the methods that will enable you to achieve your marketing objectives. They relate to the elements of the marketing mix – product, price, promotion, and place. For each objective, strategies need to be developed relating to these individual elements. Then the feasibility of the objective and its strategies is rechecked in terms of market share, sales turnover, profit margins, etc.

First the marketing strategy needs to be set out and then action plans are prepared. It is the action plans that will enable you to carry out the defined marketing strategy and achieve your marketing objectives. Chapter 7 explains how to devise marketing strategies and prepare action plans.

Define programmes

Defining programmes means defining who does what, when, where and how. It includes setting programmes for personnel, advertising and sales promotion. There may also be programmes for pricing, distribution, services and product development. Guidance on this is given in Chapters 7 and 8.

Set budgets

Objectives can be set and strategies and action plans devised, but they need to be cost-effective. If the cost of implementing your strategies and carrying out your action plans is greater than the contribution to company profits resulting from the additional sales forecast in the plan, there is no point in proceeding with them. Strategies and action plans need to be costed out and budgets need to be set. The setting of budgets defines the resources required to carry out the plan and quantifies the cost and also the financial risks involved. Budgeting is explained in Chapter 10.

Write plan

Once all of the above steps have been carried out you will be in a position to prepare the written plan. The written plan should only contain the key information that needs to be communicated. It should be clear and concise, and excessive or irrelevant detail should be excluded.

Communicate plan

If a plan is not properly communicated to those who will be implementing it, it will fail. Make sure that everyone understands the plan. Present the plan, rather than just sending a written copy in the internal mail. A plan that is not understood properly will be worse than no plan at all, because it will either be actioned incorrectly – or not at all.

The control system

It is necessary to control the implementation and review the performance of the plan. The plan must be monitored as it progresses and corrective action recommended where performance deviates from standard. This monitoring and control system should be included in the written plan. The control system should be easy to operate and should also allow for reasonable deviations from the standard before it comes into action.

Review and update

Conditions and situations will change and the plan should be regularly reviewed in the light of changing circumstances. The full implementation of the plan will be an iterative process. If major deviations occur, you may need to modify objectives, change strategies or revise schedules and budgets. An update procedure should be included in the written plan. All marketing plans should be updated and revised on a regular basis, which should be at least annually.

Chapter 11 explains how to write, communicate and update the plan.

The written plan

In order to communicate a marketing plan, it must be in the form of a written document. It is important that this should be clear and concise, simply written and easy to understand. It should not be cluttered with excessive or irrelevant detail, but should summarize information succinctly.

Some plans will be very short and others long, but a similar format with key sections should be adopted for each, although not every plan will have all these sections.

The structure of different types of plan

In this section, the structures of the different types of marketing plan are detailed. Although there is some repetition between the different types of plan, it is important to detail them all, to show that there *are* different types of plans for different purposes and not just one 'company' marketing plan.

The complete plan

The full structure would be appropriate for the full company marketing plan and other major marketing plans. Figure 2.2 shows the list of contents of a complete marketing plan.

```
– TABLE OF CONTENTS
– INTRODUCTION
– SUMMARY
– SITUATION ANALYSIS INCLUDING:  Assumptions
                                 Sales (History and Budget)
                                 Review of Strategic Markets
                                 Review of Key Products
                                 Review of Key Sales Areas
– MARKETING OBJECTIVES
– MARKETING STRATEGIES
– SCHEDULES
– SALES PROMOTION
– BUDGETS
– PROFIT AND LOSS ACCOUNT
– CONTROLS
– UPDATE PROCEDURES
```

Figure 2.2 A complete marketing plan

The basic plan

It would not be usual to include budgetary information and profit and loss account consolidation in very small plans. In this case a more basic structure would be used, as in Figure 2.3.

```
– TABLE OF CONTENTS
– INTRODUCTION
– SUMMARY
– SITUATION ANALYSIS INCLUDING:  Assumptions
                                 Sales (History and Budget)
                                 Review of Strategic Markets
                                 Review of Key Products
                                 Review of Key Sales Areas
– MARKETING OBJECTIVES
– MARKETING STRATEGIES
– SCHEDULES
– SALES PROMOTION
– CONTROLS
– UPDATE PROCEDURES
```

Figure 2.3 A basic marketing plan

The basic marketing plan would certainly be more appropriate when dealing with single markets and could be more useful in dealing with single products.

The historical plan

This is an assessment of the present position. It may be used as the first stage in the preparation of a complete marketing plan or it may be prepared for a number of different products to decide which of them have most potential for growth. The structure of this type of plan would be as shown in Figure 2.4.

```
– TABLE OF CONTENTS
– INTRODUCTION
– SUMMARY
– SITUATION ANALYSIS INCLUDING:  Assumptions
                                 Sales (History and Budget)
                                 Review of Strategic Markets
                                 Review of Key Products
                                 Review of Key Sales Areas
```

Figure 2.4 An historical marketing plan

The plan for the new product

For a new product there is no historical sales data, but there will be some data relating to the product that it supersedes or to competitors' products. If this were not the case there would be no justification for its introduction. With a completely new product, marketing research would have been carried out on market size, competition, etc. For new products it is even more important that budgetary information is shown and whether it is a separate section or not, a full justification of the reasons for the introduction of the new product must be included somewhere in the plan. This would normally be briefly included in the summary and more fully in the 'situation analysis' and 'budget' sections.

The structure of this type of plan would be as shown in Figure 2.5.

```
– TABLE OF CONTENTS
– INTRODUCTION
– SUMMARY (INCLUDING BRIEF JUSTIFICATION)
– SITUATION ANALYSIS INCLUDING:  Assumptions
                                 Sales Budget
                                 Review of Strategic Markets
                                 Review – Previous Product
                                        – Competitors' Products
                                        – New Product
                                 Review of Key Sales Areas
– MARKETING OBJECTIVES
– MARKETING STRATEGIES
– SCHEDULES
– SALES PROMOTION
– BUDGETS (INCLUDING FINANCIAL JUSTIFICATION)
– PROFIT AND LOSS ACCOUNT
– CONTROLS
– UPDATE PROCEDURES
```

Figure 2.5 A plan for a new product

Summary

There is a fixed procedure for carrying out the marketing planning process to enable you to prepare a marketing plan.

Whether you are preparing a marketing plan for a single product in a single market or a full company marketing plan, the planning procedure is the same; it is the scope of each part of the planning process that will differ. The planning process is an iterative procedure.

The written marketing plan should be clear and concise, simply written and easy to understand. It should not be cluttered with excessive or irrelevant detail, but should summarize information succinctly. Every plan should have control and update procedures and all marketing plans should be revised on an annual basis.

Following the same basic format in the preparation of all of your marketing plans will make it easier, both for yourself and for those who will read your documents.

There are a number of different types of plan including the 'historical plan', the 'basic plan', the 'complete plan' and the 'plan for the new product'.

3: The Groundwork – Market Intelligence

At the same time as the historical sales position of the company is considered, it is necessary to collect the information that will allow this to be put into perspective. To do this it is necessary to carry out both market research and marketing research. Market research is research about markets, but it is necessary to take this further and, as well as collecting information, to analyse it in the context of the marketing of the products. This is marketing research, which is research into the marketing processes as well as the markets themselves.

Why is marketing research necessary?

In today's highly competitive business environment there is no substitute for keeping in touch with the marketplace. Markets are constantly changing and so are the requirements of customers. It is easy for a company to get so involved in one market or one sector of a market that it is not able to consider the whole market for its products and may be missing potential opportunities in other markets or market sectors.

A recent study conducted by the University of Warwick's School of Industrial and Business Studies showed that 40 per cent of the US and 47 per cent of the British companies surveyed admitted that they were unclear about the characteristics and needs of their main types of customers. Only 13 per cent of the Japanese companies surveyed gave the same response. It is an accepted fact that Japanese companies have a much clearer idea of their existing and potential customers and how to reach them and they tend to target their sales and marketing efforts at those most likely to purchase their goods. This is one of the main reasons for their success in US and European markets in recent years.

In-house acquired knowledge is important, as is feedback and market intelligence from the salesforce, but they need to be supplemented by marketing research obtained from outside sources.' In the consumer goods field, the salesperson's contacts with the trade are unlikely to say enough about 'customer's' attitudes and what they find out will be limited by the contacts that they make among retailers and will not represent them all. The salesperson's selection and interpretation of what is important will inevitably be affected by the fact that information gathering is secondary to his or her primary purpose, ie to sell. Although information from salespeople and other sources will be of considerable qualitative value, it is necessary to be sure that the information on which decisions are based is as complete as possible and is representative and objective. So additional information is required, and this would be key information relating to the companies that you sell to and the industries and countries in which the product or service is being sold.

As well as information on customers, you also need information on competitors and their products. You should obtain information about how the market and your customers perceive *your company and its products*. This could include company and product image, before- and after-sales service, price and quality. You should research advertising and sales promotions to find out which methods are the most effective for your type of product or service.

In its simplest form this process is shown in Figure 3.1.

Analysis/Comparision/Evaluation

Marketing Information

In-House Experience   Salesforce Market Intelligence   Marketing Research

Figure 3.1 The collection and evaluation process

Market research is used to:

- give a description of the market

- monitor how the market changes

- decide on actions to be taken by a company and evaluate the results of these actions.

Description of the market

This is the primary purpose for which research is needed. It is of particular use to a company entering a market or launching a new product or service. In order to work out overall strategy, formulate the product or service correctly, and decide how to market it, it is important to learn all relevant information that is known about the products or services that are already in the market (if there are any), their market share, how they are distributed, who the users are, how frequently they use them, whether they only use one brand or several, and why they make their choices. A company entering a market would have to learn these things, but it is equally important for companies with established products to keep up to date with how and why their product is purchased.

Monitor how the market changes

This means periodic checking for changes in a product's or brand's share or distribution, usage or image. It is dangerous to put together plans based on out-of-date information if significant changes have occurred since the original information was collected.

Decide or evaluate potential courses of action

'Description' and 'monitoring' refer to obtaining information about the 'marketing environment'. 'Deciding on actions' relates to ways in which market research information can help a company to decide how to operate in the marketing environment. It can include the following areas:

- test marketing

- new product launches (and developments)

- acceptance testing of modified products

- promoting company image

- developing and evaluating advertising and promotion campaigns and mail shots

Methods of obtaining data for market research

Market research data consists of primary data and secondary data. Primary data is data obtained from primary sources, ie directly in the marketplace. This is obtained either by carrying out field research directly or by commissioning a consultant or market research company to carry out the fieldwork for you. Secondary data is not obtained directly from fieldwork, and market research based on secondary data sources is often referred to as desk research.

Although most large companies in the consumer goods field employ some of their own people for market research, most work is carried out by specialist market research companies. The sector has grown rapidly in recent years. Worldwide spending on market research is now in excess of £6 billion, with the UK accounting for about 9 per cent of this. Companies belonging to the Association of Market Survey Organizations (AMSO) account for 80–90 per cent of all interviewing in the UK. According to AMSO the UK market research industry is now some three times larger in real terms than it was at the beginning of the 1980s. Market research employs over 4,000 people in the UK and two-thirds are members of the Market Research Society.

The major users of market research are the food and drinks companies and other consumer goods companies. The distribution of market research expenditure in 1993 was estimated by AMSO to be as shown in Figure 3.2.

INDUSTRY	%
1 Food, drink and tobacco	25
2 Pharmaceuticals and cosmetics	13
3 Government and public services	13
4 Media and advertising	11
5 Household products	16
6 Financial services	6
7 Motoring	5
8 Retailers	4
9 Industrial products	4
10 Travel services	3
11 Other	10

Figure 3.2 Expenditure on market research in the UK in 1993

It can be seen that the proportion of the expenditure by companies marketing industrial products is very small.

Field Research

In field research the information is collected by obtaining the answers to a set of questions from a number of respondents. The sample used needs to be representative and objective. When carrying out this type of research for industrial products for industrial companies, one can be very specific in both the questions and the selection of the respondents. In the consumer field it would appear to be much more difficult, but in fact it is not as difficult as it may seem. This is because much work has been carried out on the process of sampling and relatively simple mathematical theories have been developed which work in practice.

If a sample is selected by the correct methods, every member of the population will have an equal (or known) probability of being selected. The theory of sampling is based on the concept of standard error. From a large population, there will be a large number of different ways of selecting samples. If a large number of different samples of a given size were selected, we would expect some variation in the results from these different samples. Although the different samples would not give exactly the same results, we would expect most of them to give *roughly* the same result, otherwise sampling would not be of much value.

Sampling theory tells us that results given by a very large number of samples fit into a standard pattern called the 'normal distribution'. This is a 'bell-shaped' curve with most of the results bunched together around the centre and some results tailing off in each direction. It is possible to calculate how sample results will form themselves into a normal distribution and it is therefore possible to calculate the probability that the average result from a number of samples lies within a certain range of the estimate given by one sample.

It is an important but often misunderstood fact that the error probability calculated for a sample depends only on the size of the sample itself and not on the relationship between the size of the sample and the total population. It is, however, also true that quantities for populations of many millions can be estimated from samples of only 500 or 1,000 people *if the sample is properly selected*.

If from a sample of 1,000 people you estimate that 55 per cent of the population of the country is female, there is a 95 per cent chance that the real figure will be between plus or minus 3 per cent of this figure (ie only one chance in twenty that any similar sample would produce a result below 52 per cent or above 58 per cent). If the size of the sample is increased to 4,000 the range of error would be reduced to plus or minus 1.5 per cent, ie between 53.5 per cent and 56.5 per cent. The general rule is that you have to increase the sample size by a factor or four to halve the standard error.

Sampling theory provides a safe and economical method for estimating results accurately for large populations and in practice most companies, except the largest consumer goods companies (who have their own market research departments), consult market research companies for advice on the selection of samples. The theory often has to be modified because it is expensive to take a small sample spread throughout the country. Market research companies have modified basic sampling theory to combine statistical validity with cost-effective interviewing. They use techniques such as clustering (selecting samples in a smaller geographical area) and stratification (areas are arranged in such a way that the correct proportion of relevant characteristics is included – eg rural and urban areas, North and South). There are now some very sophisticated methods of classifying geographical areas in existence and even computer programs for picking stratified sampling points.

Methods of carrying out field research

Field research can be carried out in person, by telephone or by post, and can be carried out by your own personnel or by an outside company. It is an expensive process and is best used to obtain specific information or to answer specific questions about the market. There are other methods of obtaining information in the consumer field that are part way between carrying out your own field research and desk research. These are methods such as retail audits and consumer audits.

Retail audits
The retail audit was pioneered by Nielsen in the USA. It can provide very accurate information on broad market shares, market sizes and sales trends. The principle is very simple. A representative sample of retailers is selected in a particular field (typically grocers, supermarkets, off-licences or chemists, etc). An auditor visits the retailers at regular intervals (usually twice a month). On his first visit, the auditor notes the stock of the audited items on display and in the store-room. On the next visit he notes the quantity of stock delivered since his last visit. The product sold between the visits is then calculated from the formula:

sales = initial stock + deliveries – final stock

The audit is maintained over a period of time and builds up a picture of the sales of the products and of competitive products over that time period. Setting up a retail audit is expensive and they are normally set up to be syndicable (ie the information from the audit is sold to a number of clients, most with different products). Syndication is economically possible because once the initial investment has been made in selecting and carrying out initial visits to the retailers, it is relatively inexpensive to collect data for a large number of products. Clients pay agreed subscriptions for packages of selected brands within a defined product field. The information is reported and presented in the way that the client requests it.

Consumer audits

Consumer audits use a panel of consumers to measure changes in attitudes or behaviour. This has the same effect as interviewing the same sample over and over again. It is either a sample which agreed on recruitment to be available to be contacted on all sorts of subjects or, more commonly, a panel is recruited to provide information continuously over a period. The information would need to be recorded daily otherwise it would not be remembered. So a diary is used to record purchases and consumption of particular goods. In some cases special containers are provided for used cans or cartons of the product being measured (the so-called 'dustbin check'). Consumer audits can be used to check the effect of various advertising campaigns on usage of products. They are often syndicated because of their cost.

Reactive market research with questionnaires

This is what most people associate with market research – the interviewer with the clip-board in the street. It is still the backbone of the market research industry and will probably remain so for some time, although computer techniques can be expected to become increasingly used over the next decade or so. There are in fact many ways of getting questionnaires completed. As well as personal interviews, questionnaires can also be completed by telephone interviews or as postal questionnaires. Nowadays it is quite common to find questionnaires in magazines, left in hotel rooms or given out in fast-food restaurants. It is a common method of gathering data because it is a flexible technique which is not necessarily that expensive and the questionnaires can be designed for statistical analysis by computer. It becomes a very expensive technique if the questionnaire is badly designed so that ambiguous or inadequate data is obtained.

Questionnaires need to be specific to the area to be researched and the list of questions should be designed to give as much information as possible without ambiguity. The results can be influenced by loading questions and even the order of questions can have an effect on the answers. A questionnaire needs to be designed and set out with skill by someone with knowledge of the techniques. Even then, before it is used on the full samples, it should be pilot tested on a small section of the sample. This will highlight any problems such as ambiguous questions or omissions and the questionnaire can then be modified before being used on the full samples. More detailed guidance on questionnaire design is given later in this chapter.

The methods of getting the respondent to answer the questionnaire are compared below:

Personal interviews: This can be the most comprehensive method of carrying out field research. It allows the respondent time to ponder and to answer the questions and it allows the interviewer the opportunity of asking additional questions or for clarification of a particular answer. It is, however, very costly in terms of both time and money. It involves travelling time and expenses as well as the actual time taken for the interview. There is also the time required to set up the interviews.

In the consumer field the cost is increased by the need for interviewers to work unsocial hours, because with more women working and with the requirement to contact men and women in employment rather than just the unemployed, interviewing needs to be carried out in the evenings and at weekends as well as in normal daytime hours.

Nevertheless for many purposes personal face-to-face interviewing is considered an absolute necessity. A good interviewer can form a rapport with the respondents so that they focus on the subject under discussion in a relaxed and concentrated way. He or she can lead the respondent through the questions and can also show stimuli, such as pictures, photographs or the actual product itself; this is not possible with the other methods such as telephone and postal interviewing.

Telephone interviews: Telephone interviewing is less expensive than personal interviewing because it does not incur the costs of sending interviewers out to people's homes to make the contact. People tend to be more receptive since it demands a much smaller amount of their time. This can be important in the service and industrial sector where the interviewees are businessmen or engineers at work. Such people may be reluctant to agree to a personal interview because of the time involved but would rarely refuse a telephone questionnaire *so long as it was not too long*. The respondent would initially assume that because of the cost of phone calls, the call would not be a long one. Since instant answers are demanded, it is often easier to get a full set of answers from a telephone interview than from other techniques. This must be offset by the fact that instant answers are not always the answers that would be given after due reflection.

In telephone interviewing the interviewer's voice is all-important, but other aspects of his or her personality are less important than in personal interviewing. Much greater productivity can be achieved in telephone interviewing, because there is no lost travelling time, and so many more interviews can be conducted in a day. There is also the facility for instant supervision and the correction of interviewer error. In the future there will be much more use of the 'automated telephone interview' where the answers are entered directly onto a computer for immediate processing. This method is already in operation in the USA.

Telephone interviewing is now the major method of data collection in the USA where 95 per cent of the population have telephones and it is likely to become the main development in market research interviewing in the future in all industrialized countries. The proportion of households with a phone needs to be at least 70 per cent before telephone interviewing really starts to be used in a major way. Above that level, the question of the bias on the results caused by households without a phone assumes less importance.

Postal questionnaires: This is a relatively low cost method, where the questionnaire is sent by post and the respondent is left to complete it in his or her own time. It has the advantage, as with telephone interviewing, that it does not incur the high costs involved in sending interviewers to people's homes.

It also has a number of disadvantages. There is no personal contact. Because of this, it is likely that a considerable number of questionnaires will end up in waste-paper bins. There is no way of checking whether the person it was addressed to was really the right person to ask. The respondent can scan the whole questionnaire one stage at a time. He or she can take as long as he/she wishes in formulating replies to the questions, so that postal surveys are only suitable for considered opinions and not for instant reactions. Response rates are often low and replies may come in over a long period of time, making it difficult to collate and analyse the results. Most questionnaires are sent out with a reply-paid envelope, and a reminder together with a further questionnaire is usually sent about two weeks later.

Because of the low response rates it is important to know whether the bias of those who did not reply would affect the results of the survey. For this reason it is common to check the non-response bias by telephone calls on a sub-sample.

Typical questionnaires

You will have to put together your own questionnaires based on your particular requirements, but the information given here will give you some guidelines with regard to the type of questions that you may use and the layout of the questionnaire.

Although the requirements in the consumer, service and industrial sectors are different, there are many factors in questionnaire design that are universal. The content, order and layout of questionnaires will also vary, depending on whether they are designed for personal or telephone interviews or for postal questionnaires.

The following points are important:

- the questionnaire should be specific to the area being researched and contain no irrelevant questions

- the list of questions should be designed to give as much information as possible without ambiguity

- each question should be simple and relatively short

- most questions should require a simple yes/no answer or a choice from a numbers of answers

- do not used loaded questions as these tend to give a biased result

- consider the order of questions carefully, since questions earlier in the questionnaire could influence later answers

- lay the questionnaire out in such a way that the answers can be statistically analysed easily

- avoid 'omnibus' questionnaires with a hundred questions or more – most people will not be prepared to answer more than about twenty questions

The questionnaire shown in Figure 3.3 is for a chocolate company. This company is considering launching an aerated chocolate bar similar to 'Aero' or 'Wispa'. It needs to establish a number of things relating to the market. It has already obtained information on the sales levels for Aero and Wispa in the UK from published data in reports prepared and sold by the Leatherhead Food Research Association. It wants to find out details about the typical consumer of these products: are they male or female, young or old, how often do they purchase and where do they purchase from? This will influence the type of advertising and promotion campaign that the company will use.

Area code:	Date:		Interview no:	
Please complete the following information:				
Sex Male ☐ Female ☐				
Age10–15yrs ☐	16–20yrs ☐		21–25yrs ☐	
26–30yrs ☐	31–35yrs ☐		36–40 yrs ☐	
41–50yrs ☐	51–64yrs ☐		over 65 yrs ☐	
Do you prefer	milk chocolate ☐		plain chocolate ☐	
Do you buy chocolate bars	daily ☐		twice a week ☐	
	once a week ☐		twice a month ☐	
	once a month ☐		less often ☐	
Do you buy from	sweet shop ☐		newsagent ☐	
	supermarket ☐		garage ☐	
	cinema ☐		other ☐	
Do you prefer	plain bars ☐		filled bars ☐	
When you buy plain bars do you prefer	solid (as Dairy Milk, etc) ☐			
	aerated (as Aero, Wispa, etc) ☐			
How often do you buy Aero	daily ☐		twice a week ☐	
	once a week ☐		twice a month ☐	
	once a month ☐		less often ☐	
How often do you buy Wispa	daily ☐		twice a week ☐	
	once a week ☐		twice a month ☐	
	once a month ☐		less often ☐	
Do you buy these bars for	yourself ☐		children ☐	
	wife/husband ☐		other ☐	

Figure 3.3 Questionnaire for chocolate company

The questionnaire starts with the more general questions relating to age and sex and then moves on to the types of chocolate, the types of bar, and finally to the key questions about the aerated bars. If a question such as 'Do you like aerated chocolate' had been included, it could have received the wrong response. The answer could have been No, but further investigation may have shown that the person did actually buy aerated chocolate, but either infrequently or for someone else. Most questionnaires are one or two pages in length. In many cases some questions are put on the second page of a questionnaire so that the answer does not affect preceding questions.

In service industries, the emphasis of questionnaires is usually on the quality of service as perceived by the customer. Figure 3.4 is an extract from a questionnaire from a hotel. This type of questionnaire is usually on a single page, which can be folded, sealed, and the resulting 'envelope' then either left at reception or posted.

Date of stay:				
Duration of stay: days				
Sex male ☐ female ☐				
How was reception service on arrival?				
very good ☐	good ☐	adequate ☐	bad ☐	very bad ☐
Was the bar				
very good ☐	good ☐	adequate ☐	bad ☐	very bad ☐
Did you find the restaurant service				
very good ☐	good ☐	adequate ☐	bad ☐	very bad ☐
Was the quality of food in the restaurant				
very good ☐	good ☐	adequate ☐	bad ☐	very bad ☐
Did you find room service				
very good ☐	good ☐	adequate ☐	bad ☐	very bad ☐
Was room/bathroom cleaning				
very good ☐	good ☐	adequate ☐	bad ☐	very bad ☐
Did you find staff generally				
very helpful ☐	helpful ☐	adequate ☐	unhelpful ☐	
Would you use our hotel again				
yes ☐	perhaps ☐	no ☐		

Figure 3.4 Questionnaire in hotel

In the industrial goods sector, similar types of questionnaires are often prepared, but sometimes there is a requirement for more specific information that cannot be obtained by a simple yes/no answer. Also, many companies involved in industrial goods marketing are active in markets where there are only a small number of suppliers and often only a small number of customers. A supplier of consumer goods may potentially have many millions of end customers. Many industrial goods companies have less than a thousand active customers on their files. For this reason it is common for industrial goods companies to structure questionnaires in a more general way, mixing qualitative and quantitative types of questions. Some of the major aspects on which these companies often want to have their customers' or potential customers' views are:

• Buying factors that influence them

- How they view the company and its competitors

- How they find out about new products

- Their approach to new products

Buying factors that influence them

When you buy product A, there are a number of factors that you will take into account in making your decision. Please list the factors given below, numerically, in order of priority (1 to 5)	
PRICE DELIVERY QUALITY TECHNICAL SPECIFICATION AFTER-SALES SERVICE	

Figure 3.5 Questionnaire – buying factors

How they view your company and its competitors
A similar questionnaire to that shown in Figure 3.5 could also be used to establish customers' feelings about your company. The same list of factors would be shown, but with a different question, as in Figure 3.6.

Based on the buying factors listed below, how would you rate 'Our company Ltd'?	
PRICE DELIVERY QUALITY TECHNICAL SPECIFICATION AFTER-SALES SERVICE	

Please rank as follows:
    1 – Best on the market
    2 – Better than average
    3 – Average
    4 – Worse than average
    5 – Worst on the market	

Figure 3.6 Questionnaire – image in market place

How they find out about new products

From what sources do you learn about new products in your industry? (please tick)	
TRADE ASSOCIATION MANUFACTURERS' SALES VISITS EXHIBITIONS (please state which ones) JOURNALS/MAGAZINES (please state which ones)	

Figure 3.7 Questionnaire – Awareness of new products

Their approach to new products

When purchasing a new product do you:	
(A) Contact existing users (B) Carry out your own tests (C) Seek other advice (please specify)	
In view of past experience, how long does it take for new products to be accepted into the industry:	
(A) For purchase by existing plants (B) For inclusion in specifications	
Who would specify XYZ products in your company? What approval (if any) would be required?	

Figure 3.8 Questionnaire – approach to new products

Desk research

Desk research involves the collection of data from existing sources. These sources can be:

- Government statistics

- Company information

- Trade directories

- Trade associations

- Ready-made reports

Desk research is often referred to as being cheap, since the main costs involved are the cost of the researcher's time, his/her expenses, telephone costs, and the costs of buying directories and reports. It is, however, only 'relatively' cheap in relation to the costs involved in carrying out field research. It could be a complete waste of money if the researcher chosen to do the work did not have the knowledge to work in a way that would get the required results. For this reason care needs to be taken in the selection of personnel for this task and a reasonably senior qualified person needs to be chosen to supervise the desk research. In fact, you may need to do this yourself.

Most companies use a mixture of field and desk research and it is clearly a waste of money to carry out your own research to obtain information that is already available and can be purchased in the form of a ready-made report. Many reports can be purchased for between £50 and £500. Just consider that the salary of an executive earning £25,000 a year is equivalent to £500 a week. His time would not be used cost-effectively collecting information that could easily be obtained in an existing report.

There are a number of companies that specialize in carrying out research and publishing reports. The most prominent are Keynote, Euromonitor, Mintel, and Frost and Sullivan. These organizations publish lists of reports that they have available. Euromonitor's latest list includes more than 100 directories, handbooks and statistical sourcebooks and nearly 200 reports as diverse as 'European Snack Foods' and 'The Market for Consumer Healthcare in China'. The reports include information on the market, its segmentation, the products, competition, distribution systems, and the consumer. Much information is also available on computer databases and CD-Rom.

Types of data

The marketing research information that we need for our plan is *market information* and *product information*.

Market information needs to tell us:

- The market's size – How big is it?
  - How is it segmented/structured?

- Its characteristics – Who are the main customers?
  - Who are the main suppliers?
  - What are the main products sold?

- The state of the market – Is it a new market?
  - A mature market?
  - A saturated market?

- How well are companies doing – Related to the market as a whole?
  - In relation to each other?

- Channels of distribution – What are they?

- Methods of communication – What methods are used – Press, TV, direct mail?
  - What types of sales promotion?

- Financial – Are there problems caused by:

taxes/duties
import restrictions

- Legal – Patent situation
  - Product standards
  - Legislation relating to agents
  - Trademarks/copyright
  - Protection of intellectual property (designs/software, etc)

- Developments – What new areas of the market are developing?
  - What new products are developing?
  - Is new legislation or new regulations likely?

Product information relates to your own company, your competitors and the customers:

- Potential customers – Who are they?
  - Where are they located?
  - Who are the market leaders?
  - Do they own competitors?

- Your own company – Do existing products meet customers' needs?
  - Is product development necessary?
  - Are completely new products required?
  - What would be the potential of a new product?
  - How is your company perceived in the market?

- Your competitors – Who are they?
  - How do they compare with your company in size?
  - Where are they located?
  - Do they operate in the same market sectors as you?
  - What products do they manufacture/sell?
  - How does their pricing compare with your own?
  - What sales/distribution channels do they use?
  - Have they recently introduced new products?

There are four main areas of published data that can be used in marketing research to provide the market and product information required. These are:

- Market reports

- Company information

- Product and statistical information

- Consumer information

Market reports

Market information and market reports are the most comprehensive types of market research information. They look at all aspects of the market including companies, products, customers and trends. They present an overview of the whole market and allow a company to assess where it is positioned in the market.

The key areas covered by market reports are:

- A history of the market

- The structure of the market

- The size of the market

- Data on major companies in the market

- Market trends

- Distribution channels

- Recent market developments

- Future market developments

Reports may be on a single market, a single market sector, or on a number of related markets. Reports may be obtained from companies already mentioned or they may be obtained from specialist research or consulting organizations such as the Leatherhead Food Research Association (for food industry reports) or Jaako Pori (for pulp and paper industry reports).

Company information

We need information on other companies in order to investigate potential customers and distributors and also to monitor our competitors and potential competitors.

Company information is of two types:

- Directory information

- Financial information

Directory information gives key data on companies. This includes names, addresses, telephone numbers, trade-marks, details of directors, and Who owns Whom. They usually list companies operating in particular markets.

The main trade directories such as Kompass Directories and Kelly's Directories cover all of the larger companies and include a great deal of information with a detailed analysis of activities and products. Kompass have a wide range of directories covering many foreign countries as well as their UK directories. There are also a wide range of more specialized directories covering single industries or industry sectors (such as the chemical industry, offshore oil and gas and the textile industry). These directories are often not as detailed as the main trade directories and often they only show the name, address and telephone numbers of companies, with a brief list of products, but they do have the advantage of being specific to their industry. Directory sources are detailed at the end of the book under 'Useful Addresses'.

Financial information relates to the trading performance of a company and is normally an analysis of a company's financial accounts for one or more years. By law all UK companies have to file copies of their financial accounts with Companies House. The information must include:

- The directors' report and accounts

- The annual return

- The mortgage register

- The memorandum and articles of association

- Changes in registered office or name

- Details of any bankruptcy proceedings

The amount of information required from small companies is not the same as that required for large companies and it is quite common for small companies to give no details of turnover. This can be a problem in analysing information where small companies are involved.

Copies of companies' financial accounts can be obtained by requesting a copy from Companies House. More detailed information on individual companies can be obtained from companies such as Dun & Bradstreet.

A sensible way of obtaining this kind of information for an

industry is to obtain a Business Ratio Report for that industry from a company such as ICC Business Publications who specialize in producing such reports. These reports analyse industries by examining the results of the leading companies in the industry. The sample usually covers from 50 to 150 companies. In the reports firms are often grouped into subsectors in order to give a thoroughly comparative analysis. The reports include up to 26 tables of ratios, such as return on capital, return on assets, profit margin, and stock turnover. The companies are ranked according to ratio performance. Additionally, averages are calculated for the whole industry and, where applicable, each subsector. Information for these reports is derived from the annual audited accounts of companies filed at Companies House. In each report the tables of ratios are preceded by an informative commentary and followed by individual financial and directory profiles on all companies included in the report.

There are currently over 150 business ratio reports available. These reports can also be useful in relating your company's performance to others in your own industry. Using the ratio approach, you can compare the performance of your company with the performance of major competitors.

Product and statistical information

In many countries government statistics are a useful source of information. These relate to business activity in the country itself, as well as to details of imports and exports of products and commodities. Another useful source of international trade and production statistics is information produced by United Nations Organizations such as the Food and Agriculture Organization (FAO).

To find your way around such statistics, it is necessary to have a basic understanding of the main coding and classification systems used for economic activity and products. There have been major changes to these systems in the last few years and a good guide to the development of and relationship between the systems is given in *Standard Industrial Classification of Economic Activities 1992* published by HMSO.

The system that is most commonly used by directories or financial reports classifies companies into industries by relating their main activities to the official standard industrial classification (SIC) codes. The codes in use in the UK are the SIC codes (revised 1992). (Care should be taken to differentiate from the US SIC codes which are different and are used by American companies such as Dun & Bradstreet.)

The UK SIC codes are based on NACE Rev 1 which is an EU regulation requiring the use of common codes throughout the EU, but where it was thought necessary a fifth digit has been added to form subclasses of the NACE Rev 1 four digit classes. Thus SIC(92) is a hierarchical five digit system. At the highest level of aggregation, SIC(92) is divided into 17 sections each denoted by a single letter from A to Q. These sections are given in Table 3.1.

Table 3.1 SIC Codings

Section	Industrial Classification
A	Agriculture, hunting and forestry
B	Fishing
C	Mining and quarrying
D	Manufacturing
E	Electricity, gas and water supply
F	Construction
G	Wholesale and retail trade
	Repair of motor vehicles, motorcycles and personal and household goods
H	Hotels and restaurants
I	Transport, storage and communication
J	Financial intermediation
K	Real estate, renting and business activities
L	Public administration and defence
	Compulsory social security
M	Education
N	Health and social work
O	Other community, social and personal service activities
P	Private households with employed persons
Q	Extra-territorial organizations and bodies

Some sections are, in turn, divided into subsections (each denoted by the addition of a second letter). The letters of the sections and subsections do not need to be part of the SIC/NACE codes because they can be uniquely defined by the next breakdown, the divisions (denoted by two digits). The divisions are then broken down into groups (three digits), then into classes (four digits) and in some cases, again into subclasses (five digits). An example is given below:

Section D   Manufacturing (divisions 15–37)
Subsection DB   Manufacture of textiles and textile products (divisions 17 and 18)
Division 17   Manufacture of textiles

Group 17.4	Manufacture of made-up textile articles, except apparel
Class 17.40	Manufacture of made-up textile articles, except apparel
Subclass 17.40/1	Manufacture of soft furnishings

In 1989 the United Nations Statistical Commission agreed a Central Product Classification (CPC) which provides direct links to the Harmonized Commodity Description and Coding System (HS). The HS, known generally as 'tariff numbers', replaced the Customs Co-operation Council Nomenclature (CCCN) in 1988 and is the coding system used for trade worldwide.

Only the first eight digits of the HS code are of major importance. The first two digits denote the chapter, the next two digits denote the part of the chapter, the third set of two digits denotes the section and the fourth set of two digits denotes the subsection. If further digits are used, the ninth digit is a special subdivision for use in a particular country and the tenth and eleventh digits are for non-EU countries.

Thus the coding HS 841360 41 0 is broken down as follows:

Chapter	84	Machinery, mech/elec appliances and parts
Part	13	Pumps for liquids
Section	60	Other rotary PD pumps
Subsection	41	Gear pumps
National	0	National breakdown (used for statistics)

The EU preferred a product classification that was more akin to the industrial activity classification and devised the Classification of Products by Activity (CPA). One of the uses of the CPA is to code the PRODCOM lists. PRODCOM is a new system that was agreed in 1992 to harmonize the collection of statistics throughout the EC. PRODCOM stands for Products of the European Community. All EU countries are now using this system and will be publishing statistics from 1995 onwards. The UK was the first country to start publishing statistics in May 1995 – the information is called 'UK Markets' and replaced the 'Business Monitor PAS/PQ Series'. The information is in the form of reports that are published annually – quarterly for some of the most popular products. The reports provide Total Market Data (UK production, or more precisely, UK manufacturer sales, exports, imports and net supply to the UK market in both value and volume terms as well as average price) on some 4,800 products. UK

Markets are published by Taylor Nelson AGB and contain PRODCOM data collected by the Central Statistical Office covering all of the UK's producers and manufacturers and import/export data. They are available from HMSO Books.

Consumer information

A considerable amount of data is available relating to consumers and consumer goods. In fact no major consumer goods company could survive for long without carrying out very specific marketing research and analysis. Such information is of value not only to companies operating in consumer markets, but also to those operating in the industrial market supplying goods to the manufacturers of consumer goods.

Consumer goods markets differ from industrial markets by having a large number of customers who are all different. Since advertising and selling on a national scale is expensive consumer goods suppliers target sections of the consumer market for their product.

Consumer markets are usually segmented by the characteristics of their consumers and this involves the analysis of a group of factors. Generally, consumers are classified by:

- socio-economic group

- age

- sex

- occupation

- region

The classification system developed by Research Services Ltd is the most commonly used system for determining socio-economic groups in the UK. It divides consumers into six broad groups, as shown in Table 3.2.

Table 3.2 Consumer classification by socio-economic groups

Group	Social Status
A	Upper middle class
B	Middle class
C1	Lower middle class
C2	Skilled working class
D	Working class
E	Lower class

Other classifications can be used to classify family types, housing types and area groups. These include the classification system for area of residence called ACORN (A Classification Of Residential Neighbours) developed by CACI market analysis group, and the alternative residential-based classification of consumers called (PIN) (Pinpoint Identified Neighbourhoods) developed by Pinpoint Analysis Ltd.

Table 3.3 shows the main Acorn groups used in the UK.

Table 3.3 Consumer classification by Acorn groups

Category	
A	Agricultural areas
B	Modern family housing, higher incomes
C	Older housing of intermediate status
D	Older terraced housing
E	Council estates – category I
F	Council estates – category II
G	Council estates – category III
H	Mixed inner metropolitan areas
I	High status non-family areas
J	Affluent suburban housing
K	Better-off retirement areas
L	Unclassified

Each ACORN and PIN group can be further subdivided into subgroups.

In the consumer goods industry, advertising research is also important. It is essential to know how much your competitors are spending and what they are spending it on. Advertising research can also assess which media channel is most used by customers of a given product.

How to plan your marketing research

We have now covered all of the main methods and data available for marketing research, but it is important to plan how you will carry out the research in your particular case to obtain the right information for your plan. You will not need to use all of the methods and all of the types of data in every case. Obviously the scope of the work will be much more comprehensive if you are preparing an overall marketing plan for all of your company's products in all markets than if you are preparing a plan for one product in one market only. Figure 3.9 shows the principle of planning marketing research.

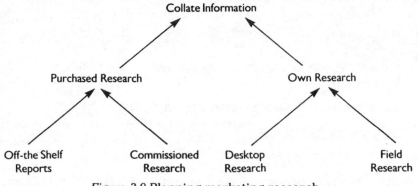

Figure 3.9 Planning marketing research

Much time, effort and cost is wasted by starting marketing research projects without defining the objectives.

The key steps to carrying out the marketing research are as follows:

- Define the objectives

- Decide what information needs to be obtained

- Decide the best way of obtaining it

- Collect the data

- Analyse the data

The objectives

The objectives must be clearly defined. This should include the time-scale that is necessary for completion of the work to fit in with the time-scale of preparation of the overall marketing plan. If the plan concerned equipment to be sold into the chocolate and confectionery industry then the objective of the research would be to gather information about this industry including its size, major companies involved, growth patterns, etc. Time should not, however, be wasted gathering wider-ranging information about the food industry in general.

The information required

A list should be prepared, detailing all of the information required. This must be a complete list of everything needed, because it is extremely costly to have to go back later to collect additional information because it was not considered in the first place.

How to obtain the information

This is one of the most crucial decisions to be taken. It involves deciding who will obtain the required information and how it will be obtained. The options are:

- Use own staff
- Use outside market research company
- Carry out field research
- Carry out desk research

Only the very largest companies have market research professionals on their staff. A project involving more than a minimal amount of fieldwork is best carried out by a professional. The cost of carrying out such a project could easily be as high as £20,000, which may sound a great deal, but is, in fact, probably value for money. In marketing research you get what you pay for. It should be noted that in the UK, government grants are often available for marketing research projects.

In practical terms large amounts of fieldwork are rarely necessary in the capital goods field, but are quite usual in the consumer goods field.

If the requirement is for a small amount of fieldwork and a large amount of desk work, then it is usually carried out in-house. The staff chosen to do this work must be capable of understanding what they are doing. It should not be seen as just a clerical job and should only be entrusted to someone who will be able to understand the methods of marketing research and the full objectives of the project. That person may, of course, use less senior staff to assist him, or her. Many such projects fail to obtain the depth of information required because they are entrusted to unmotivated junior staff.

In the capital goods industries, the small amounts of fieldwork required are often carried out by the field sales staff in the course of their normal duties. The person carrying out the project will prepare a form to be completed by field sales staff based on their individual knowledge of their territory and their customers.

Collecting the data

Collecting the data involves using the methods and the data sources detailed earlier in the chapter. The names and addresses of some key sources of information are listed at the end of the book.

Analysing the data

The data on its own is of no use to anyone: it needs to be verified and analysed. Verification really means being sure that the information has been collected in a logical and unbiased way. It should be representative and needs to be as complete as possible. The assumptions used in interpreting the data need to be stated.

The analysis of the data needs to be carried out by your marketing professional (this may be you personally). The analysis of the data is only as good as the understanding of the person carrying out the analysis.

Information may be available from published reports, giving market size. Where this information is not directly available an approximation can often be made from statistical data. UK government statistics give much information on British industry, and import/export data is also useful for certain products. If you are the only UK manufacturer of your product, import information, if available, would give you valuable information relating to the sales in the UK by your overseas competitors.

The best source of this information comes from PRODCOM statistics. In the UK these are published annually as reports. When all EU countries publish their own PRODCOM statistics, it will be possible to obtain reports from all EU countries giving production, imports and exports of any of the products covered. If you were a footware manufacturer, you could obtain reports analysing the PRODCOM statistics for footware in each EU country and compare production in each country, exports and imports within the EU and exports and imports outside the EU.

In other areas, in-house knowledge is crucial. How many people do you know in sales and marketing who can tell you that as a rule of thumb they calculate potential sales of their product as one machine for every so many thousand tonnes of industry capacity? Many people have worked out such rules and they are crucial in calculating the total potential market for a product.

If you know that the average capacity of a sugar refinery in Europe is, say, 100,000 tonnes of sugar per year, and you find out that sugar production in the UK is 1.4 million tonnes and in Denmark it is 600,000 tonnes, you know that it is reasonable to assume that there will be 14 refineries in the UK and 6 in Denmark. Equally, if you know that such a refinery usually uses 20 of your machines, you know that you have a potential market of 280 machines in the UK and 120 machines in Denmark.

If you want to be able to use marketing research data to the full, you need to be able to work out some similar rules of your own. Your estimates may be only an approximation, but they will still be far more accurate than guesses.

Now that you have completed the external market research, it is time to move on to collecting the historical data that is available in-house.

Summary

There is no substitute for keeping in touch with the marketplace. Markets are constantly changing and so are the requirements of customers. In-house knowledge needs to be supplemented by marketing research acquired from outside sources.

Market research data consists of primary and secondary data. Primary data is obtained directly in the marketplace by carrying out field research, whereas secondary data is obtained by desk research.

Field research can be carried out through personal interviews, telephone interviews or postal questionnaires. Desk research involves the collection of data from existing sources such as government statistics, company information, trade directories, trade associations, or ready-made reports.

The marketing research information required for marketing planning is market information and product information.

There are a number of systems for classifying companies, products and consumer types. Companies are classified by activity using Standard Industrial Classification (SIC) codes. The classification of goods has been simplified by the use of the Harmonized Commodity Description and Coding System (HS) and in the EU the PRODCOM system is now used to produce statistics. Socio-economic groupings for consumers can be classified by the Research Services Ltd system or by the ACORN or PIN grouping systems.

Marketing research must be planned and it is important to set objectives, list the information required and decide how to obtain this information before proceeding with the project. The data obtained must then be sensibly analysed and presented so that the best use will be made of it in the marketing planning process.

4: Historical Data – Collecting and Analysing Information About Your Own Company and Products

In addition to the external market research, your own company has a wealth of data that is invaluable in the preparation of a marketing plan – whether it is an overall plan or one for a single product or market. In fact the problem is more likely to be that there is too much data so that you cannot easily see which information is the most important. It is also likely that much data will not be available in the right form. You may have overall sales data, but not data itemized for individual product lines or market segments. As you sift through and sort the information you may also be able to see how systems could be set up that would make it easier to obtain the relevant information in the future.

The historical data relevant to the preparation of a marketing plan is of two types:

- Sales/Order data

- Other data

Technically speaking, the difference between order intake data and invoiced sales data is the delivery time of the product. Order intake data is self-explanatory and refers to the orders placed with the company. Invoiced sales are the invoiced values for those goods when they leave the factory, ie sales out of the door.

If a product has a delivery time of six months or more, then the difference between order intake and invoiced sales could be significant and a considerable amount of this year's order intake would become part of next year's invoiced sales. In the time-scale of a marketing plan, this would be significant and it should be made clear which figures are being used. If a product has a short delivery time – say three to six weeks – the difference between order intake and invoiced sales is so small that it really does not matter which type of figure is used. This may be true in many cases, but there may still be instances where customers place large orders ahead of a price increase for delivery over a considerable period of time. These factors will not only affect the marketing plan itself, but will also have an impact on the cash flow predictions in the finance plan.

Order intake data is often available in a more comprehensive form than sales data and sales departments are usually more interested in an order analysis than a sales analysis.

Where possible sales figures should be used, but if order intake figures are the only figures available in the detail that you require, use them with caution and try to smooth out any anomalies that may be present. In other words, try to convert them as nearly as possible to the sales figures. It is, after all, the figures for invoiced sales that are important to a business – orders are only orders until they are converted to sales. It is sales, or more correctly invoiced sales, that bring in money to the company.

An important question to consider is how far back it is sensible to go when analysing sales figures. Some companies have sales data going back 10 or even 20 years, but it really makes no sense to go so far back. Even five years is a long time ago in marketing terms and is not strictly relevant, because markets change, products change and the marketing environment changes as well.

A marketing plan should include two or three full years' historical data as well as the current forecast for the year in which the plan is put together. The figures for the current year should also show the year-to-date figures.

The sales or order intake figures on their own will not give a full picture of a company's performance. They need to be compared with budgets. The profitability of the sales also needs to be quantified.

The figures will be of most use in marketing planning if they are presented in such a way as to reflect the market segments that the company is operating in.

What is market segmentation?

Market segmentation is a very important concept in marketing and in marketing planning.

Different customers have different needs. They do not all require the same product and they do not all require the same product benefits. Even with an individual product, not all customers will buy it for the same reasons. Unless your objective is always to sell your product at the lowest price (and there are very few companies that can do this and stay in business for long), you need to find groups of customers who will buy your product for other reasons, such as quality, service or additional product benefits. Market segmentation allows you to consider the markets you are actually in and the markets that your company should be in.

You need to be able to split your customer base up into groups of customers who all have similar needs. Each of these groups constitutes a market segment. Once you recognize the differences between these segments you can start to make and sell products that best meet the specialized needs of customers in individual segments. You should then be able to sell your product at an acceptable price, which is not necessarily the lowest price. You can also aim your promotion and advertising specifically at profitable segments of the market.

There are many different ways to segment markets. In theory, you could say that there are as many market segments as there are individual customers, but in practice this would make no economic sense.

It is sensible to consider ways of segmenting markets separately for consumer goods and services and for industrial goods and services.

Market segmentation for consumer goods and services

In these industries it is usual to segment markets based on different ways of classifying the end-user. In Chapter 3 we looked at these methods of classification which separate consumers by socio-economic group, age, sex, occupation, or region.

The main ways of defining segments are:

- by social class – upper middle, middle, lower middle, etc

- by demographic classification – sex, age, education, marital status, etc

- by geographic area – north, south east, south west, etc

- by geodemographic category – agricultural, council estate, multi-ethnic area, suburban housing, retirement housing etc

- by psychographic category based on personality traits or lifestyle – student, modern girl, young executive, etc

Market segmentation for industrial goods and services

In the marketing of industrial goods and services the customer is usually another company or a government department. The number of customers and potential customers is more likely to be ten thousand than ten million (as could be the case with consumer goods) and could be only a few hundred in cases such as suppliers to power stations, coal mines, etc.

The main ways of defining segments here are:

- by geographical area
- by industry or industry subsector
- by product
- by application
- by size of end-user
- by distribution channel – distributor, equipment manufacturer, end-user

Segmentation can also be based on:

- order size
- order frequency
- type of decision-maker

The key to market segmentation is to let the marketplace segment itself, because the individual segments exist independently of the company and its products. They will not change to accommodate the company or its products. The buying patterns that cause segmentation are rational and should provide an insight into increasing market share within a segment. It can often be the case that a natural segment provides a market niche for a company that enables it to trade without direct competition from its major competitors in that segment.

How to present the figures

Depending on the scope of the plan, the sales/order data may be split up into separate tables geographically, by product, by industry or under all of these categories. In fact, any sensible way of segmenting the figures can be used. Figures may also be given separately in value terms and as numbers of units.

It is usual when producing tables of historical data to extend the form layout to include columns for the years which the marketing plan will cover. The columns for future years remain blank at this time as the current task is to record historical and current sales data, but it makes it easier later on to project sales figures so that comparisons can be made and trends can be seen. Such tables can easily be prepared as spreadsheets on computer programs such as Excel or Lotus 1-2-3. Figures 4.1 and 4.2 show examples of how sales figures can be presented.

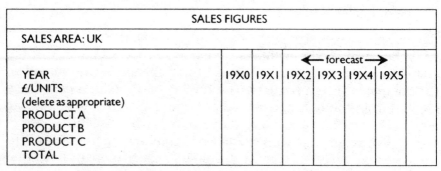

SALES FIGURES						
PRODUCT LINE: PRODUCT A						
YEAR £/UNITS (delete as appropriate) UK OTHER EUROPE NORTH AMERICA ASIA REST OF WORLD TOTAL	19X0	19X1	19X2	19X3	19X4	19X5

Figure 4.1 Sales figures presented geographically

SALES FIGURES						
SALES AREA: UK						
YEAR £/UNITS (delete as appropriate) PRODUCT A PRODUCT B PRODUCT C TOTAL	19X0	19X1	19X2	19X3	19X4	19X5

Figure 4.2 Sales figures presented by product

These methods of presenting historical data can be used for consumer goods, industrial products, or services. With any product there can be seasonal trends, such as increased business before the end of the financial year or before the implementation of your price increase. In the case of products such as Easter eggs, Christmas cards and Christmas crackers, the seasonal element would clearly be considerable and would affect production, storage, finance, distribution, cash flow – in fact all elements of the business. There is therefore some merit in presenting additional figures for individual years showing orders and sales on a monthly basis (see example in Figure 4.3). This factor is probably more significant in the consumer and consumer durable goods markets than with industrial goods.

SALES FIGURES FOR 19X2													
SALES AREA: UK													
£/UNITS (delete as appropriate) PRODUCT A PRODUCT B PRODUCT C TOTAL	JAN	FEB	MAR	APR	MAY	JUN	JUL	AUG	SEP	OCT	NOV	DEC	19X2

Figure 4.3 Sales figures presented by month

We will now consider how the figures could be presented for a hypothetical company selling equipment into the dairy industry. Its major markets are the UK, Europe and the USA. Its sales figures for the last two years and forecast for the current year are shown in Figure 4.4.

THE EQUIPMENT MANUFACTURING COMPANY LTD						
SALES FIGURES – ACTUAL						
PRODUCT LINE: ALL PRODUCTS			←forecast→			
YEAR (all values in £k)	19X0	19X1	19X2	19X3	19X4	19X5
UK	200	240	230			
OTHER EUROPE	950	950	950			
USA	300	350	450			
REST OF WORLD	150	160	170			
TOTAL	1600	1700	1800			

Figure 4.4 Presentation of actual sales figures

The figure shows details of order intake for the last two years and the forecast for the current year. Although year-to-date figures would also be known, for the sake of clarity these have not been shown. These figures are as they were taken from the order book and, since prices will have been increased in line with inflation, these figures do not truly reflect the increase in business during this period of time. If the year-to-date figures suggest that the original forecast for the current year is too high or too low, re-estimated figures should be used.

Inflation and exchange rate fluctuations are two major problems that can affect the credibility of figures when they are being interpreted in marketing planning.

Figure 4.5 shows the same set of figures as Figure 4.4, but this time they have been adjusted for inflation. It is assumed that price increases over the period were 7 per cent per year. To return everything to 19X0 values the 19X1 figures have been divided by 1.07 and the 19X2 values by 1.07 × 1.07.

This gives a very different picture from the first set of figures and it shows the importance of adjusting for inflation. We are deceiving ourselves if we do not make this adjustment, because what we are looking for are real trends. It is important that the adjustments are based upon removing our price increases, which may be more than, the same as, or less than published inflation figures.

The adjusted figures show an overall real decline in sales of 2 per cent in total over the three-year period. This is a long way from the gradual increase of 12.5 per cent that appeared to be the case from Figure 4.4.

THE EQUIPMENT MANUFACTURING COMPANY LTD							
SALES FIGURES – INFLATION ADJUSTED							
PRODUCT LINE: ALL PRODUCTS							
				←— forecast —→			
YEAR (all values in £k)(at 19X0 prices)	19X0	19X1	19X2	19X3	19X4	19X5	
UK	200	224	201				
OTHER EUROPE	950	887	830				
USA	300	327	393				
REST OF WORLD	150	150	148				
TOTAL	1600	1588	1572				

Figure 4.5 Presentation of Inflation-adjusted sales figures

Further analysis of the figures is also enlightening:

- There has been a steady decrease in order intake in Europe in real terms to 13 per cent below the 19X0 figure

- There have been no real increases in order intake from the UK and the 'rest of the world'

- The USA is the one bright spot, where order intake is up by 31 per cent over the period – but even this could be an illusion if this gain is purely a result of exchange rate variations

The problems of allowing for inflation and the effect of exchange rate variations are significant enough on historical figures where inflation rates and exchange rates are already known. In forecasting it is even more difficult, because one has to guess what future inflation and exchange rates will be. One way to avoid these problems is to present figures separately based on the numbers of units sold rather than their values. This gives a clear indication of whether sales of a particular product are increasing or decreasing. In the presentation of historical data, you should always include information showing the volume sales trends as well as value figures. Figure 4.6 shows how this type of data can be presented.

THE EQUIPMENT MANUFACTURING COMPANY LTD							
SALES							
PRODUCT LINE: FILTERS							
			←—— forecast ——→				
YEAR (numbers of units)	19X0	19X1	19X2	19X3	19X4	19X5	
UK	30	32	40				
OTHER EUROPE	15	18	45				
REST OF WORLD	5	5	15				
TOTAL	50	55	100				

Figure 4.6 Presentation of sales by number of units

If many different products are manufactured, then it may well be useful to carry out the above analysis for several major products. It is important that the amount of product sold justifies such a detailed analysis and you should not try to analyse and draw conclusions from very small quantities.

Whether as values or as numbers of units, figures must be analysed sensibly. If the overall order intake figure is £2M, it is not meaningful to highlight an increase in order intake from Malta of 500 per cent if the initial figure was £1,000 and the final figure £5,000.

Key major areas should be picked out in a logical way and footnotes should be added as required. If major markets are the USA and Japan, these should be highlighted and separated out in some way. It is illogical to talk about 'the Far East' if 98 per cent of Far East sales are to Japan. In this case highlight Japan, and the rest of the Far East orders would be included under 'rest of the world'.

The information put together so far gives a detailed view of how historical sales have increased or decreased over the last three years. It does not indicate whether the sales were on budget or if they were profitable. This information is of considerable importance. The variation of sales in relation to budget will indicate how good the forecasting has been and may suggest that there are other problem areas that need to be addressed. (The sales organization may be inadequate or the product may be nearing the end of its life cycle.)

The *profitability* of these sales is paramount. If the product is not profitable it is important to find out why this is and to decide on a plan of action to rectify the situation.

The figures need to be obtained and presented in a way that will show sales against budget and profitability.

THE EQUIPMENT MANUFACTURING COMPANY										
SALES FIGURES										
SALES AREA: UK										
YEAR	19X0			19X1			19X2			COMMENTS
	SALES	FORE-CAST	GROSS PROFIT	SALES	FORE-CAST	GROSS PROFIT	SALES	FORE-CAST	GROSS PROFIT	
	£K	£K	%	£K	£K	%	£K	£K	%	
FILTERS	50	40	40	80	60	40	95	90	40	
VALVES	50	40	30	80	60	30	85	100	30	
COMPONENTS	100	100	60	90	110	60	70	90	60	
TOTAL	200	180	47.5	250	230	44	250	280	42.2	

Figure 4.7 Presentation of sales figures against forecast showing gross profit

A more complete format for presenting data is shown in Figure 4.7. This would be expanded in the plan to include forecasts for sales and gross profit. It shows how important it is to compare sales figures with forecasts and to analyse profits and margins. In this case the company is increasing sales of its least profitable products while sales of its most profitable products decline. It has also not been forecasting this situation.

I would add a note of caution here. A company having figures as shown in Figure 4.7 would certainly have to look into the situation in detail. Nevertheless, the relationships between costs, sales and profits are not always what they seem. The disproportionate allocation of overheads to a product can make it seem less profitable than it really is and marginal business can be worth having even at reduced margins. More information on costing techniques and budgeting is given in Chapter 10.

The plan for the home market

When analysing figures for the home market, or indeed when putting together a marketing plan purely for the home market, it is sensible to analyse small figures. These figures may well be for areas where sales are low because of unsatisfactory sales coverage and the potential may well be much higher.

Let us assume that the figures in Figure 4.8 are for a new product introduced in 19X1. From these figures we may surmise that the product was first introduced in the South West in 19X0, but was not introduced into other areas of England until 19X1 and into Scotland and Northern Ireland in 19X2.

THE EQUIPMENT MANUFACTURING COMPANY				
SALES FIGURES				
SALES AREA: UK PRODUCT: MILK MONITORING UNITS				
YEAR (all values in £k)	19X0	19X1	19X2	19X3 (forecast)
SOUTH WEST	10	20	50	100
SOUTH EAST		5	10	20
EAST ANGLIA		5	10	30
MIDLANDS		10	20	30
NORTH WEST		10	20	30
NORTH EAST		5	15	30
WALES		5	10	20
SCOTLAND			10	20
N. IRELAND			10	20
TOTAL UK	10	60	155	300

Figure 4.8 Sales figures for a new product for the home market

We could further analyse the sales in the various areas and compare these figures with the size of the dairy industry in the particular areas. The figures clearly show the most rapid and sustained growth in the South West which is quite likely to be the case with equipment sold into the dairy industry. If the equipment had been a product sold only into heavy industry then we would have expected the major markets and major growth to have been in the Midlands and the North.

What if it is a completely new product?

When preparing a marketing plan for a completely new product, it is likely that there will be no historical sales data at all. There is, of course, the situation where the product is superseding another product and in such cases historical data for the superseded product should be used. Due note should however, be taken of changes to the specification of the new product which may broaden its application.

Even if there is no historical data relating to the product, some market research would have been carried out to determine market size, competition, etc, and to estimate the potential market for the product. The methods used are the same as those used to make projections of the potential market for any product, and this is covered in Chapter 6.

Market performance

To put the information that you have collected into context, you need to compare the data for a number of years and also to compare your figures with the market information produced using the methods shown in Chapter 3.

You need to ask a number of questions:

- What is the total size of the market for your products/services in the geographical area chosen (eg UK, Western Europe)?

- How has the market changed over the last three years?

- What is your market share for each product group/market segment?

- How has it changed over the last three years?

- Who are your major competitors?

- What were their sales for the last three years in the geographical area chosen?

- What were their market shares in these markets for the last three years?

From the historical sales data that you have now put together in this chapter, you will be able to compare your actual sales figures with figures for the total market and you will probably also have some data on your competitors' sales which will enable you to build up a more complete picture.

In Chapter 6 you will see how this data can be built up into projections and how to set marketing objectives for the plan.

The use of databases

The power and use of computers and the spread of information technology is obviously increasing at an amazing rate. The hardware in use now would have been barely conceivable even ten years ago. Software has become much more 'user friendly'. There are now standard packages for office automation that can be customized for individual company use. Many manufacturing companies have installed MRP (materials resource planning) systems based on a computer which, in effect, acts on a database of the company's current and expected order intake and sales. These systems normally include a sales and a finance package with the facility to extract information from the database for the purpose of sales analysis. Further useful analysis can be carried out if it is possible to segregate customers by SIC codes and to split order intake related to these specific industries.

Every single order has to be allocated the SIC code relevant to the industry that it is being sold into and the analysis work is carried out on the codes. Information can be obtained based on values and numbers of units of different products sold into different industries.

Even now, if your company does not yet have an office automation system or the system does not include the parameters that you want to measure, it is still possible to use computers with database programs to analyse data. Most companies of even medium size in developed countries have a computer system nowadays and these systems should provide at least some information on invoiced sales. In some cases, however, it may mean that someone will have to go back through order data for the last three years and extract the relevant information to put it manually into a database.

There is no excuse for companies – however small – not to keep some information on databases for use in marketing planning, because even if the company's main computer does not provide the information, such databases can be prepared by the sales and marketing department itself and can be run on ordinary PCs. Nowadays, high quality fast PCs with large hard disks and colour screens can be purchased for little more than £1,000. They can be linked by means of a network, so that information can be shared. On a network, the main file is held on a fileserver and can be updated by any user, so that it is always up-to-date. These PCs can be used with office software packages such as Microsoft Office or Lotus Software Suite. These packages include word processing, spreadsheet and database programs and information can be transferred between the different programs.

A computer database can be a powerful tool and it is not necessary to have a detailed knowledge of computers to use one. In its simplest form you can use the database functions of spreadsheet programs such as Lotus 1-2-3 or Microsoft Excel. These allow you to sort data alphabetically or by date or number. The next stage is to use the associated database – Access (with Excel) or Approach (with Lotus 1-2-3).

The difference between a database and a spreadsheet is that a spreadsheet is essentially two dimensional and a database is three dimensional. The possibilities of sorting and analysing data are therefore greater with a true database.

Before setting up your database you need to decide *all* of the parameters that you want to record – not just for now, but for the future. At the moment you may only be interested to know how many units were sold over the last three years and not their size or colour, but it is wise to construct the list of data for the database to include other parameters that may be needed for future analysis work. A database is effectively a set of individual entries of data that can be sorted by the computer in a variety of ways. It can sort just as easily on 'colour' as on 'size of unit' or 'customer industry code'.

With the transparency of modern software, it is quite possible to enter data in an Excel spreadsheet and then regularly download it into an Access database to process it further. It is also possible to maintain a dynamic link between the two programs so that when data in one is changed, the other is automatically modified.

Before you import spreadsheet data into a database you should ensure that the format of the data is appropriate for a database table. For example, be sure that the data has the same fields in every row and that the information in each column is of the same data type.

Once a database has been installed, it should be continuously kept up-to-date so that it can be analysed as and when required by the marketing department.

Of course, the advantage with office automation systems is that this data is part of the normal input at the time that an order is entered into the system and does not have to be entered twice.

Most databases will only present the final data as lists or at best as a spreadsheet. In marketing, presentation quality is all-important and in your marketing plan you should use all possible means to prepare the most professional-looking and clearly presented tables or graphs. Remember that pictures always emphasize a point more dramatically than figures and with the low cost of colour printers, colour can also be used to good effect.

The advantage of integrated office software packages is that they usually include a high quality presentation program. Graphs can be prepared in Excel, but Microsoft Office includes the Powerpoint presentation package and data and images can be transferred between the two.

Examples of information in an Excel spreadsheet and how it can be enhanced by the use of the Powerpoint presentation package are shown in Figures 4.9 to 4.12.

SALES FIGURES				
PRODUCT LINE:STANDARD FILTERS				
(all values in £k)				
YEAR	19X0	19X1	19X2	19X3
UK	200	250	250	300
OTHER EUROPE	950	1000	950	1000
USA	300	380	410	500
REST OF WORLD	150	170	190	200
TOTAL	1600	1800	1800	2000

Figure 4.9 Spreadsheet in Excel

SALES FIGURES
PRODUCT LINE - STANDARD FILTERS

YEAR	19X0	19X1	19X2	19X3
(all values in £k)				
UK	200	250	250	300
OTHER EUROPE	950	1000	950	1000
USA	300	380	410	500
REST OF WORLD	150	170	190	200
TOTAL	1600	1800	1800	2000

Figure 4.10 The same spreadsheet imported into Powerpoint

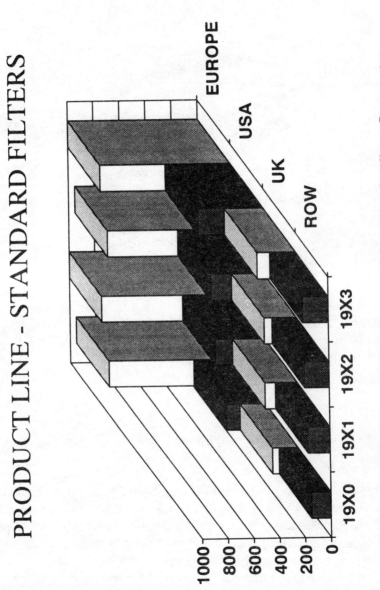

SALES FIGURES
PRODUCT LINE - STANDARD FILTERS

Figure 4.11 Example of the same information shown graphically on Powerpoint

SALES FIGURES
PRODUCT LINE - STANDARD FILTERS

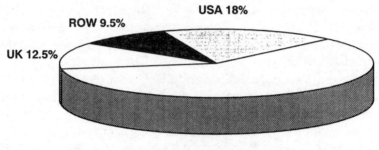

Figure 4.12 A further example of Powerpoint

Summary

Your company is a valuable source of data for use in your marketing plan. This historical 'in-house' data needs to be added to the more general market information collected using the techniques outlined in Chapter 3.

You should present data to show:

- invoiced sales

- numbers of units sold

- sales compared with budgets

- gross profits

The information should be collected and presented in such a way as to reflect the key market segments into which you sell your products. For the products and markets covered by your plan you should collect and present information going back two or three full years, together with this year's forecast sales.

The historical information should be entered in a format that includes space for forecast data as well, even though this would be left blank at this stage. If seasonal sales are a significant part of total sales, the information should also be presented to show monthly sales throughout the year. You should indicate the effect of inflation/price increases and exchange rate fluctuations on the figures you present. You should also present figures for the number of units sold, because this is a measure that removes inflation.

You should not include individual figures that are too small to be relevant. More detail and smaller individual figures may be more relevant in a plan for your home market than in an overall plan.

Although there will probably be no historical data available for a new product, market research would still be carried out to determine the market size, gather information on the competition, and estimate the market potential.

The information collected needs to be put into context in relation to market information collected as outlined in Chapter 3 and the information year on year needs to be compared and contrasted.

Company databases can provide useful information for this internal market research and, once set up, they will continue to provide such information for future marketing planning.

5: Situation Analysis – Strengths and Weaknesses – How Do You Compare With the Competition?

Completing the marketing research and collecting the historical data about your company and its products is only the first step. You need to analyse this information and to present it in a form that can be used for planning. Before you can decide on your marketing objectives and future strategies, you need to understand clearly the present position of your company and its products in the marketplace. Situation analysis is a process which helps you to do this:

- It reviews the economic and business climate

- It considers where the company stands in its strategic markets and key sales areas

- It looks at the strengths and weaknesses of the company – its organization, its performance and its key products

- It compares the company with its competitors

- It identifies opportunities and threats

The results of this analysis are included in the plan under the headings:

- Assumptions

- Sales

- Key products

- Strategic markets

- Key sales areas

It is only when the process of situation analysis is complete that marketing objectives can be set. The results of the analysis will also be used in deciding strategies and tactics. Situation analysis is therefore the key to the preparation of any marketing plan.

Assumptions

The first part of the situation analysis involves reviewing the economic and business climate. This is because all marketing plans must be based on a set of assumptions. It is these assumptions that will decide what can and what cannot possibly be achieved. They should be few in number and should relate only to key issues.

If it is possible for the plan to be implemented regardless of an assumption, then that assumption is not necessary and should be removed from the plan. The only assumptions included in the plan should be the key planning assumptions which would significantly affect the likelihood of the marketing objectives being achieved. They would normally relate to external factors over which the company has no control. They could include such things as:

- The market growth rate – are markets expanding? Is recession likely?

- The exchange rate – what effect would a declining or appreciating pound have on the plan? What are the major currencies that need to be considered?

- Interest rates – are they likely to rise or fall? How will this affect business?

- Government plans or legislation – is there any planned government legislation that will impact on the plan?

- Employment/recruitment – how easy/difficult is it to recruit and retain personnel?

The assumptions will be carried forward to the written plan, but they will be constantly reviewed, both at the planning stage and during the course of implementation of the plan, in the light of changing circumstances.

Sales

Company performance

The company performance in terms of sales and profit for key products in key areas will be known from the historical sales data collected in Chapter 4. You now need to look at this data and analyse it. It will be presented under the section 'sales' in the marketing plan. In addition, you will need to consider trends in sales:

- What are the trends in the sales of your product/service?

- How do sales/profits compare with targets year on year for the last three years? How good is your forecasting?

- What amount of your business is new business?

- How does this compare with the growth in repeat business?

- How do your company business ratios compare with those of your competitors?

- How does your company's sales growth compare with the growth of key competitors?

- What is your estimated market share for key products in key markets? How has this changed over the last three years?

- Why do customers buy from you?

- Why do customers not buy from you?

- Do you record lost sales and find out why they were lost?

- How do your prices compare with those of your main competitors?

You now need to consider your key market segments both geographically and by industry or industry segment. These are your 'strategic markets' and 'key sales areas'.

Strategic markets

Strategic markets are 'market sectors' or 'industries' rather than geographical markets. If the marketing plan is for a complete range of products in all industries, your strategic markets will be the main industries into which the product is sold. If the marketing plan is for that one product in only one industry, strategic markets will be key application areas in that one industry.

Strategic markets for a dairy equipment manufacturer would be:

- dairies

- cheese-making plants

- butter-making plants

- yoghurt production plants

- milk tankers

- milking parlours

For a package holiday company, the strategic markets could be:

- UK holidays

- premium package tour market

- mass package tour market

- charter flights

For your strategic markets, you need to detail information on the size of each market, growth rates, and your own position in each market now and in the future.

Key sales areas

Sales areas in the context of a marketing plan means geographical areas. The way that you split your sales area will depend on how you define your markets within your company.

The home market or UK market would normally be separated out in one of the following ways:

- North of England/South of England; or

- Between two and twelve regional areas; or

- In counties

Overseas markets could be classified as:

- Europe/Americas/Asia/Africa/Australia; or

- Western Europe/USA/Rest of World; or

- Western Europe/USA/Japan/Rest of World

There may be reasons other than geographical for markets to be classified together. The company may have subsidiary or associated companies in some countries and may wish to record details of these companies separately. For a company with subsidiary companies in West Germany, the USA and Australia, the markets could be classified as: Intercompany/Other Europe/Other Americas/Asia/Africa.

The home market

Trying to put together a world-wide plan for a product can be a daunting task if you have never attempted a marketing plan before and it is probably best to prepare a plan for your home market first, since this is the market with which you will be most familiar and it is also the market for which information will be most readily available.

Although we normally consider only major or 'key' sales areas in a marketing plan, the home market is something of an exception, in that it is usual to detail all areas of the home market, however small their current or projected order intake levels may be.

As detailed above, there are many different ways in which the UK market can be divided. It is usual to separate Scotland and Northern Ireland from other areas. This is because of their size in relation to population and their distance from the major industrial centres of England and Wales. The same would be true, but for different reasons, if your company were based in Scotland or Northern Ireland.

The rest of the UK (England and Wales) would be subdivided into a number of areas, depending on the sales coverage envisaged. A detailed résumé of the past and present situation would be recorded for each area and future potential would also be noted. Key account customers in the area would be listed, together with any other relevant data.

Overseas markets

The overseas markets are somewhat different. There are more than 160 different countries in the world and because of extreme fluctuations in market conditions, not even the most ambitious marketing person would consider selling to them all.

There will be key overseas sales areas and these should first be clearly identified. Having done this, the next thing to decide is whether you can sensibly write one marketing plan for the product in all overseas markets or whether regional plans should be prepared. If your company exports 70 per cent of its turnover and half of these exports go to one market – say the USA – it would clearly be sensible to prepare one plan for the USA and one plan for the rest of the world. Most companies could quite happily prepare only one overall plan for all overseas markets.

In preparing your plan for overseas markets, you should first identify the key overseas sales areas for your product. This will include both major existing and major potential sales areas.

If your product is aimed at high technology industries, your key overseas sales areas would probably be:

West Germany/France/Italy/Scandinavia/Benelux/USA/Japan

If your product is for use in desert regions the key sales areas would probably be:

USA/Australia/South Africa/Saudi Arabia/Gulf States/North Africa

You should only select *Key* areas and not try to cover every area.

Let us assume that you have selected ten key areas. Split these areas into logical groups – say Europe, North America, and Rest of the World. Put the group with the largest current order intake first and do a résumé of the past and present situation in each area and the future potential. Notes on the distributor/agent coverage (if applicable) and the competitive situation in that market should also be included.

SWOT analysis

The key process used in situation analysis is SWOT analysis. SWOT stands for:

'**S**trengths and **W**eaknesses as they relate to our **O**pportunities and **T**hreats in the marketplace.'

The strengths and weaknesses refer to the company and its products whereas the opportunities and threats are usually taken to be external factors over which the company has no control. SWOT analysis involves understanding and analysing your strengths and weaknesses and identifying threats to your business as well as opportunities in the marketplace. You can then attempt to exploit your strengths, overcome your weaknesses, grasp opportunities and defend yourself against threats. This is one of the most important parts of the whole planning process. SWOT analysis asks the questions that will enable you to decide whether your company and the product will really be able to fulfil your plan and what the constraints will be. It is important that you are totally honest when you list your strengths and weaknesses.

Strengths and weaknesses include not only the strengths and weaknesses of your company and its products, but also those of your competitors, since these will determine how successful you will be in implementing your plan.

It should also be noted that something that could be a strength in one way could be a weakness in another: being a small company will probably give a flexible approach to customers (strength), but the company will lack the advantages of organization and economies of scale of manufacturing and purchasing of a large company (weakness).

Some of the 'opportunities' and 'threats' will be developed from the 'strengths' and 'weaknesses' of the company and its products, but most will be derived from the marketing environment, developments in key market segments and, of course, the competition. An opportunity is something that can be exploited to your advantage, so it could be one of your strengths or one of your competitor's weaknesses. It could equally well be an opportunity caused by an expanding market or by the opening up of a new market. Threats can be actual or potential threats at some time in the future. A threat could be posed by low-priced competition, but it could equally well result from planned government legislation or from a potential fall in a particular exchange rate.

In carrying out a SWOT analysis it is usual to list the strengths, weaknesses, opportunities and threats on the same page. This can be done in several different ways. The four headings can be put across the top of the page and four vertical lists prepared. A better effect can be obtained by segmenting the page into four squares and entering strengths and weaknesses in the top squares and opportunities and threats in the bottom squares, as shown in Figure 5.1.

STRENGTHS	WEAKNESSES
OPPORTUNITIES	THREATS

Figure 5.1 Presentation of SWOT analysis

The number of individual SWOT analyses will depend on the scope of your plan. First you should carry out a SWOT on your company and its organization. You should also do the same for your main competitors and for the products, geographical areas and market segments covered by the plan. With key products, a list should also be made of the features of the products and the benefits that these features give to the customer. For the geographical areas (key sales areas) and the market segments (strategic markets), our main interest is in the opportunities and threats. The main SWOT analyses will be included in the relevant sections of the written plan.

Examples of what constitutes strengths and weaknesses, opportunities and threats, and the types of questions that you might ask in carrying out a SWOT analysis, are given in the following sections.

Company organization

Before you consider your product and markets, you need to understand how your company and its organization will affect your business. You must list its strengths and weaknesses and consider any threats and opportunities.

The *strengths* of a company and its organization could be such things as:

- For a large company – it is well known in the marketplace – it has good resources

- For a small company – it can be more flexible

- It has a good internal sales organization

- It has a good external sales organization

- It has a good distribution network

- It has a captive sales network covering the UK

- The company manufactures in the UK

- The fact that the company has various industry standard approvals

- It has a 'quality' image

Weaknesses could be such things as:

- It is a small company – competitors are larger and well known in the marketplace

- It has an inadequate internal sales organization

- It has an incomplete or inadequate external sales organization

- The fact that the sales manager needs to be replaced

- There is an inability to recruit satisfactory staff

- It has a bad image for 'quality'

- The company lacks or has an inadequate distributor network

- It has an inadequate or non-existent service network

- It has only one manufacturing centre and this is in a high labour cost area

- It has long or unreliable deliveries

- Its competitors have a better or more complete distributor network

- Its competitors have a captive sales network through overseas subsidiaries

- Its competitors have industry standard approvals that it does not have

Opportunities could be such things as:

- The company has been taken over by a company that is a large potential customer for its products

- The company has recently been merged with another company giving it the advantage of economies of scale in manufacturing

- Recent investment has given the company an edge over its competitors

- The pound sterling has fallen, making the company's products more attractive in overseas markets and overseas competitors more expensive in the UK

Threats could be such things as:

- Its largest customer has recently taken over one of its major competitors

- The bulk of its overseas business is sold in US dollars

- Foreign competitors are building a new factory in the UK

An example of a company SWOT analysis is given in Figure 5.2.

STRENGTHS	WEAKNESSES
Large company Part of large UK group Size – the biggest in UK Good image – high profile Good resources – financial 　　　　　　 – technical 　　　　　　 – marketing 　　　　　　 – R & D	Factory location Little known overseas Lack of flexibility Recently restructured
OPPORTUNITIES	THREATS
To exploit overseas markets To develop new products To further develop economies of scale	Japanese competition High UK interest rates

Figure 5.2 Company SWOT analysis for large company

The SWOT analysis will be used in the development of the marketing plan. All four sections are of use to us. The strengths can be further exploited by the company in its advertising and sales promotion, the weaknesses give a list of issues that need to be addressed for improvement. The opportunities need to be exploited in the plan, and contingency plans can be prepared to counter the threats.

In addition to carrying out a SWOT analysis on the company, you can use the technique on the sales organization itself and also to appraise your staff and sales personnel. This will allow you to understand where you have strengths and weaknesses in these areas. Typical questions that you might ask are given below.

Structure

• Do you have a clear organization chart for your department and your company? Is this freely circulated throughout the company?

• Has the company structure changed to meet changing markets or is it fixed and likely to remain so?

• Do you have too few or too many staff in key areas?

Staff

• What are the strengths and weaknesses of each member of your staff?

• How often do you hold sales meetings?

• Do you and your staff need training? If so, in what areas?

• Do your staff have job descriptions? Are these regularly updated?

• What is your rate of staff turnover? Is it high or low?

- Is the relationship between the members of different departments good?
- Do your staff know the objectives of the company and of the department?

Sales personnel

- Do your sales personnel have sufficient knowledge of the operation of other departments?
- Do you have a proper training programme for your key sales personnel?
- Are their commissions/bonuses sufficiently performance-related?
- Do your staff work to sales targets on a weekly/monthly/yearly basis?
- Do you carry out regular individual staff appraisals?
- If you died/left who would take your place? Is there a proper succession plan for key people in the sales organization?
- When did you last attend a training course?
- When did you last test the product knowledge of your sales personnel for: your products?; your competitors' products?
- How do you measure/appraise individual performance?
- How do your salespeople spend their working day? Have you analysed this?
- Are your salespeople deployed by geographical area or by product?

STAFF APPRAISAL		
Name/Position	Strengths	Weaknesses

Figure 5.3 Staff appraisal form

You should now carry out a complete appraisal of the strengths and weaknesses of all of your staff. It would be appropriate for individual managers to carry out the appraisals for their own staff. Figure 5.3 shows an example of a form to be used for this staff appraisal.

The results of the individual appraisals would remain confidential, but the key information would be used in the SWOT analysis of the sales organization.

A typical SWOT analysis for a sales organization is given in Figure 5.4.

Again, the list of weaknesses needs to be addressed and at the departmental level it is easier to propose the appropriate course of action than it is at company level. The strengths and opportunities can be exploited.

STRENGTHS	WEAKNESSES
Good sales management team	Many new staff – need experience
Large field salesforce in UK	Staff training required
High calibre of sales personnel	Limited database info available
Good distributor network in UK	Sales manager needs replacing
New modern offices	Limited coverage of export markets
Have industry specialists	
OPPORTUNITIES	THREATS
To expand market share in existing markets	No logical successor to sales and marketing director
To develop new markets	Competitors expanding field salesforce
	Overseas competitors have better distribution in overseas markets

Figure 5.4 SWOT analysis for a sales organization

The competition

Your company performance needs to be compared with the performance of your major competitors. The threat of competition usually only comes from a handful of companies and you should be able to identify them.

You need to define:

- Who your major competitors are

- What products and services they offer

- What their strengths and weaknesses are

Major competitors

You should only consider major competitors, and not every single competitor that you have. You should initially compare the financial position of your company and your competitors using published information such as company annual reports. Additional information can be obtained from companies that specialize in supplying financial information (see Chapter 3).

Before tabulating the information you need to define the headings that you will use and you must make sure that you are comparing information expressed on the same basis. Many individual items of financial information and ratios can be used. A selection of key ones are shown in Figure 5.5.

The same comparison should be carried out, not just for the last financial year, but for the last two or three financial years. This will then give a clearer picture of what is happening in the competitive marketplace – which companies are increasing turnover and whether this is being achieved profitably or not. It will also enable you to set standards for your industry and you can compare your results with these.

COMPETITOR COMPARISON	Financial year:		
	YOUR COMPANY	COMPETITOR A	COMPETITOR B
Sales turnover			
Trading profit			
Depreciation			
Operating profit			
Profit before tax			
Total fixed assets			
Stocks			
Debtors			
Total current assets			
Creditors			
Short-term loans			
Total current liabilities			
Total current assets			
Long-term liabilities			
Shareholders' funds			
Number of employees			
Profit per employee			
Ratios			
Return on capital			
Return on sales			
Sales per employee			
Stock turnover			
Debtor days			
Creditor days			
Current ratio			
Quick ratio			

Figure 5.5 Competitor financial comparison

A financial comparison tells you a lot about the market. It tells you who the key players are, and which companies are increasing their market penetration. The companies that are most successful do not achieve this success for no reason; they achieve greater success because of some activity that they are carrying out better than others. You need to isolate these factors of success and compare them with the same activities in your company. They would be factors such as:

• The image of the company in the marketplace

• Its organization/sales ability

• Its financial position

• Pricing

• Distribution

• Speed and reliability of delivery

• Product quality

• Value for money

• After-sales service

• Advertising

Not all of these factors will have the same influence in terms of assuring success. The factors therefore need to be weighted in terms of their relative importance.

The competitor analysis in Figure 5.6 gives you a matrix to show how you compare with the competition overall and with regard to each of the key success factors.

COMPETITOR ANALYSIS				
Give rating: 1 = lowest (poor/bad), 10 = highest (good) Multiply rating by weighting factor				
KEY AREAS	WEIGHTING FACTOR	YOUR COMPANY	COMPETITOR A	COMPETITOR B
Company image	2			
Organization	1			
Premises	1			
Location	1			
Sales ability	5			
Product quality	4			
Technical spec.	2			
Product range	2			
Prices	4			
Distribution	3			
Delivery	4			
After-sales service	3			
Advertising	2			
Total				

Figure 5.6 Competitor analysis

MARKET SHARE ANALYSIS			
Market: UK Product: Widgets			
	19X0	19X1	19X2
Market size (£m) Market size (m. units) Your sales (£m) Your sales (m. units) Your market share (£%) Your market share (units %)			

Figure 5.7 Presentation of details of company market share for one product in one area

Depending on the scope of your plan you should now compare your sales with the sales of your major competitors by area, market segment or industry over the last two or three years. This will enable you to see trends which will be taken into account in your planning. With consumer and service industries, much information is published on market shares in different geographical markets. This is as true for chocolate bars as it is for cars. For specialized industrial goods such information is not so easily found. Competitor information by geographical area is often available in annual reports which will split sales turnover into UK sales and a number of key export territories such as the USA or Europe. Market share is a difficult thing to estimate accurately. It is fair to say that *most companies overestimate their market shares.*

Sales of your own company and of major competitors can be compared and presented in the format shown in Figures 5.7 and 5.8. This information should be prepared for each market, market segment and product that will be covered by your plan.

COMPARATIVE MARKET PERFORMANCE						
Market: UK Product: Widgets						
	19X0		19X1		19X2	
	Sales (£m)	Market share (%)	Sales (£m)	Market share (%)	Sales (£m)	Market share (%)
Your company Competitor A Competitor B Competitor C Total						

Figure 5.8 Comparative market performance

Having presented and analysed all of the information on the competition and their performance in the marketplace, a SWOT analysis can now be carried out on each of the main competitors. This can be presented as shown in Figure 5.9. Since your company's strengths can be your competitor's weaknesses and your competitor's opportunities can be threats to you, it is important that you label which is which. It may be obvious to you, but not to someone else reading the SWOT analysis later.

Key products

You should examine technological and competitive factors relating to your main products. Remember that you do not sell a 'product' to a customer, you sell a 'benefit' that the product gives to the customer.

Their strengths	Their weaknesses
Competitor A:	
Part of large group	Outdated product
Good resources	No room to expand existing factory site
Relatively large market share	
Large captive customer in same group	
Competitor B:	
Small company – low overheads	Not well known in marketplace
Flexible working practices	New product – not yet well established
Low price level	Little after-sales support
Competitor C:	
Good quality – cheap product	Product is imported from Italy
	– no local service backup
Opportunities (for us)	Threats (to us)
Competitor A:	
Our new product can gain market share at their expense	They have the resource to develop new products quickly
	They have the reputation and image to launch it successfully
Competitor B:	
	Low prices are affecting traditional pricing levels
Competitor C:	
We could also import some product for low priced sector	If sales increase they will be able to support backup service

Figure 5.9 Competitor SWOT analysis

You should look at your major products and list their key features and the benefits that derive from these features. Do the same for your competitors' products. Remember: FEATURES MEAN BENEFITS. Do not say that your product is small, say that because it is small, it is easily portable. Do not say that it is new, say that because it is new, it incorporates the latest technology. Figure 5.10 shows how to complete a features and benefits chart.

FEATURE	MEANS	BENEFIT
small		easily portable
microprocessor control		less likely to go wrong
LED display		easy to read
chip update service		customer gets improvements as we develop them
nationwide service network		good and quick service

Figure 5.10 Features vs benefits chart for an electronics product

You should also carry out a SWOT analysis on your product compared with your competitor's products. Typical questions you may ask are:

- How do our prices compare with those of our main competitors?

- What would be the effect of raising/lowering our prices by 10 per cent?

- Is our product larger/smaller than our competitors' products?

- What technical aspects are better/worse than our competitors' products?

- Does our product have patent protection?

- Do our competitors' products have patent protection?

- Does our product comply with the industry standards?

- Do our competitors' products also comply with the industry standards?

- Is our product made from better/worse materials than competitors' products?

- Is it of light/heavy construction?

- Is it easier/more difficult to maintain than competitors' products?

A small company manufacturing a new type of colour television set in the UK might produce the SWOT analysis shown in Figure 5.11.

STRENGTHS	WEAKNESSES
Futuristic design Patented Clear screen Neat profile Lightweight Fits into stacked music centre units	Limited range – 2 screen sizes Market as yet undeveloped Trade name little known Relatively high price

OPPORTUNITIES
To exploit market for users who
   want one overall entertainment
   centre
	THREATS
	Low priced imports

Figure 5.11 SWOT analysis for new television product

Summary

Situation analysis allows you to present the data relating to your company, products and sales in a form that can be used for planning. It reviews the economic environment and the business climate as well as areas of your company and its operations that you can influence. It considers your key products and your position in your strategic markets and key sales areas. It relates and compares your company and its products with your competitors.

The most important process in situation analysis is the SWOT analysis which involves looking at strengths and weaknesses as they relate to opportunities and threats in the marketplace. The strengths and weaknesses refer to the company and its products whereas the opportunities and threats are usually taken to be external factors over which the company has no control. SWOT analyses should be carried out with regard to your company and its organization/performance, your main competitors and also, for all of the products, geographical areas and market segments covered by the plan.

The results of the situation analysis are included in the marketing plan under the headings:

- Assumptions
- Sales
- Key products
- Strategic markets
- Key sales areas

6: Marketing Objectives – The Aims of the Plan

Now that we have identified our key strengths and weaknesses, the opportunities and threats to our business, and made assumptions about outside factors that may affect our business, we are in a position to set our marketing objectives. This is the key step in the whole process of preparing a marketing plan.

What is a marketing objective?

Objectives are what we want to achieve; strategies are how we get there. There are therefore objectives and strategies at all levels within the company. They cascade down from the top levels of corporate management to the lowliest levels of the company.

At the top we have the company corporate objectives. These are the goals of the company as laid down in the strategic and corporate plans and will include short-term, medium-term and long-term objectives. From the company's corporate objectives will come the company's corporate strategies. These will lead in turn to the objectives at the next level down, ie at the functional level. These objectives will include the production objectives, personnel objectives, finance objectives, distribution objectives and marketing objectives. Objectives and strategies are therefore interlinked and one leads logically to the other.

A marketing objective concerns the balance between products and their markets. It relates to *which products* we want to sell into *which markets*.

The means of achieving these objectives, using price, promotion and distribution, are marketing strategies. At the next level down there will be personnel objectives and personnel strategies, advertising objectives and advertising strategies, etc. There will then be tactics, action plans and budgets – all to enable us to achieve our objectives.

Marketing objectives relate to any of the following:

- selling existing products into existing markets

- selling existing products into new markets

- selling new products into existing markets

- selling new products into new markets

Marketing objectives must be definable and quantifiable so that there is an achievable target to aim towards. They should be defined in such a way that, when the marketing plan is implemented, actual performance can be compared with the objective. They must be expressed in terms of values or market shares, and vague terms such as increase, improve, or maximize should not be used. A marketing plan can be for any number of years ahead. There will be different final objectives for one-, three- and five-year plans, but the objectives at year one and year three should be the same in each case.

To increase sales in all areas is not a sensible marketing objective, because it is not quantified and therefore cannot be measured. Any increase in sales would achieve this objective.

The following are examples of marketing objectives:

- To increase sales of the product in the UK by 10 per cent per annum in real terms, each year for the next three years

- To increase sales of the product worldwide by 30 per cent in real terms within five years

- To increase our market share for the product in the USA from 10 per cent to 15 per cent over two years

- To introduce our new product in the UK and to achieve profitable sales of £500,000 per annum within a five-year period

Although marketing plans can cover any period of time, it is usual for companies to have long-term marketing plans covering a period of three or five years, and more detailed one-year plans for the year ahead. In all plans marketing objectives for the following should be set:

- Sales turnover for the period of the plan by product and market segment

- Market share for the period of the plan by product and market segment

- Gross profit on sales

There may be other objectives that are relevant to a particular business. The plan may cover only one product and the market segments could be geographical or by industry. It could be for a new product which is not expected to break even for several years after its launch. There will, of course, be some marketing objectives that a company will set based on the opportunities identified in the SWOT analyses.

The product portfolio

Since marketing objectives relate to *products* and *markets* it is important to understand your present position with regard to both before setting the objectives of your marketing plan. From the situation analysis outlined in Chapter 5 you understand more about your company, products, competitors and markets. You know your historical sales by market segment and your estimated market shares. The SWOT analyses have highlighted strengths and weaknesses, opportunities and threats. Nevertheless, it is necessary to carry out further analysis of the products in your portfolio before you can sensibly set your marketing objectives. These objectives will relate to future levels of sales and market shares and these will be in large part dependent on whether you have the right mix of products in your portfolio. A company with only one product in its portfolio is vulnerable in the same way as a company that only sells its product/s in one market segment.

Product life cycle

In predicting future sales it is important to differentiate between a new product which may be destined for rapid growth and a mature product which may be being superseded in the market. The growth and decline of all products follows a life-cycle curve which can be represented as in Figure 6.1. The slope of the curve and the length of time represented by the different stages will vary, but all products will move through a similar curve.

At different stages in a product's life cycle the company should make changes to its strategies for advertising, pricing and distribution to adapt to changing market circumstances. When a product is introduced, growth is slow. At this stage advertising is concentrated on making the customers aware that the product exists. As it starts to become established repeat purchasing takes place and sales increase. There is then a period of rapid growth. Competitors start to enter the market and their sales promotion increases the market's awareness of the product and this expands the market further. At this stage changes are necessary in the company's advertising

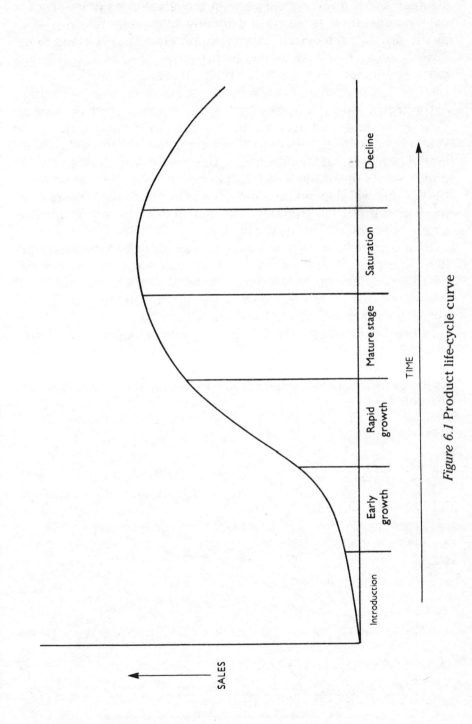

Figure 6.1 Product life-cycle curve

strategy and it now concentrates on the advantages of its product over competitors' products. Eventually sales start to slow down as the product achieves its maximum potential. Further additional growth stages can be achieved by bringing out improved versions of the product, by expanding the range of product available, and by the development of new markets for the product. Even with these extra growth stages, the product will eventually start to plateau. This is the mature stage, which may last for a short time or for years. Eventually, more competitors enter the market, which is no longer growing, and the product reaches its saturation stage. At this point sales of the product will start to decline, although the speed of the decline will depend on whether you or your competitors have the better product. Ultimately, the product will be superseded by a new product and will be dropped.

With a product like a new ice-cream flavour or a skate-board, the life cycle may be only one year. A product such as a motor car or a bicycle may be in fashion for several years. Some industrial products such as filters, valves or heat exchangers can remain virtually unchanged for a decade and still sell well.

In estimating future sales, it is therefore important to be able to assess where your product is on the life-cycle curve. If it is a mature product you need to decide whether it is possible to extend its life by further development of the product itself or by finding new markets for it.

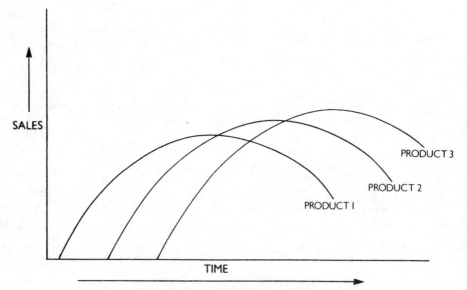

Figure 6.2 A product portfolio

Most companies do not sell just one product. If you have a portfolio consisting of a number of products, they will each have their own individual product life cycle. The ideal product portfolio will have a range of products at different stages in their life cycles so that balanced growth can be achieved and risks can be minimized. Figure 6.2 shows a typical product portfolio. The product portfolio should be reviewed on a regular basis.

Relative market growth rate and share

In Chapter 5 we looked at calculating market share, but we have not yet discussed the importance of market share. In any market the price levels of the major players tend to be broadly similar. No-one wants to sell products at a lower price than necessary because this means giving money away, but equally if your prices are set too high, the competition will undercut you. For this reason, in a stable market, the price levels of the major players will gradually move together. If two companies are selling the same product at the same price, it does not necessarily mean that they are both making the same level of profit. If one company has a very large market share, it will benefit from economies of scale and will have lower costs. If the other company has a low market share, its costs will be higher and its profit margin will be lower. If, as the market for the product begins to decline, one company decides to drop its price to try to retain its level of sales, the other will have to follow. The company with the highest market share and therefore the highest profit margin will be more able to withstand such a price war. The company's market share for the product, relative to that of its competitors, also indicates its ability to generate cash. It is therefore important not only to increase sales, but also to increase your market share. Your aim should be to try to achieve market dominance wherever possible.

Before you can decide on the potential for growth of sales you need to analyse which products are your key products – now and for the future. We have already looked at the concept of the product life cycle. There is also another method of considering your product portfolio.

Cash flow is the most important factor in considering your product portfolio, and your company's ability to generate cash will be dependent, to a large extent, on the degree of market dominance that you have over your competitors. Some years ago the Boston Consulting Group developed a matrix for classifying a portfolio of products according to their cash absorption or generation based on relative market shares and relative market growth rates. The 'Boston Matrix' is now widely used by companies to consider their product portfolio. Products are colourfully described as:

STARS – high market share/high market growth (cash neutral)
CASH COWS – high market share/low market growth (cash generation)
QUESTION MARKS – low market share/high market growth (cash drain)
DOGS – low market share/low market growth (cash neutral)

Relative market share is the ratio of your market share to the market share of your biggest competitor. It indicates the level of market dominance that you have over your competitors. If your market share is 20 per cent and your biggest competitor has a market share of 10 per cent the relative ratio would be 2:1. This is clearly a more satisfactory position than one where you both have a 20 per cent market share (relative ratio of 1:1) or the very unsatisfactory position where you have a 10 per cent market share and your major competitor has a market share of 20 per cent, giving him the relative advantage. Nevertheless it is important to know your relative position, because this will suggest particular strategies that you will adopt and these strategies will differ depending on your relative market share. A high relative market share is normally taken to be greater than a ratio of 1:1 compared to your largest competitor.

Market growth rate is important for two reasons. In a fast-growing market the sales of a product can grow more quickly than in a slow-growing or stable market. In increasing sales, the product will absorb a high level of cash to support increasing advertising, sales coverage, sales support and possibly even investment in additional plant and machinery. The definition of a high market growth rate will depend on the type of market you are in, but for the purpose of marketing planning, it is normally taken as 10 per cent or more.

The products are entered into the quadrants of a matrix as shown in Figure 6.3.

Question marks can be either newly launched products which have not yet fulfilled expectations, or products that are declining and need further evaluation as to their long-term viability.
Dogs have low market share and are generally unprofitable. These

products would be considered as those that could be dropped from the product portfolio.

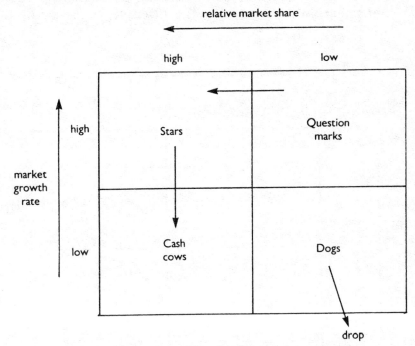

Figure 6.3 Ideal product development sequence

Stars have a high cost in spending on marketing and research and development, but also contribute considerably to profits. They are broadly speaking neutral from the point of view of cash generation.

Cash Cows are mature products with a high market share, but low market growth. They generate high profits and require only a small amount of marketing investment and no research and development spending to keep them where they are.

For a company with six products the present position could be as shown in Figure 6.4. Product 1 contributes 15 per cent of the company's sales volume, it has a relative market share of 2:1 to its largest competitor and it is in a fast-growing market that is expanding at a rate of 15 per cent per year.

Although the matrix shows the present position with regard to the company's product portfolio, it gives no indication of how this is changing. The changing situation can be seen clearly if the figures for sales volume of these products two or three years ago are shown on the same diagram as the current figures. Figure 6.5 shows this in tabular form.

This information can now be entered on a complete portfolio matrix showing the changes over the three years preceding the

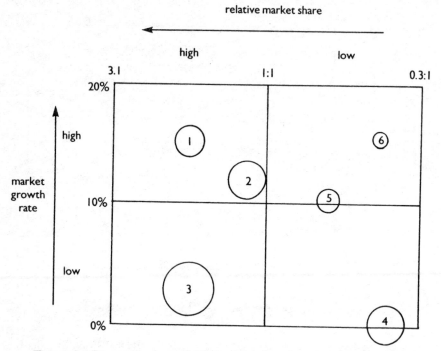

Figure 6.4 Example of portfolio matrix showing present situation

	PERCENTAGE OF TOTAL SALES		MARKET GROWTH RATE		RELATIVE MARKET SHARE	
PRODUCT	19X3 %	19X0 %	19X3 %	19X0 %	19X3	19X0
PRODUCT 1	15	10	15	12	2:1	2.8:1
PRODUCT 2	20	15	12	10	1.2:1	0.8:1
PRODUCT 3	30	36	2	2	2:1	2:1
PRODUCT 4	20	35	2	0	0.4:1	0.1:1
PRODUCT 5	10	5	10	10	0.55:1	0.45:1
PRODUCT 6	5	0	15		0.4:1	

Figure 6.5 Data for use in product portfolio matrix

new plan that is being prepared (Figure 6.6). Much more can be seen from this matrix than from one just showing the present position. Sales of product 1 have increased, both in real terms and also as a percentage of the company's sales turnover. Nevertheless, the market has grown at a faster rate and the company's relative market share has fallen.

Product 2 has registered an increase in sales which has been above the market growth rate and has increased its relative market share and changed from being a 'question mark' to being a 'star'.

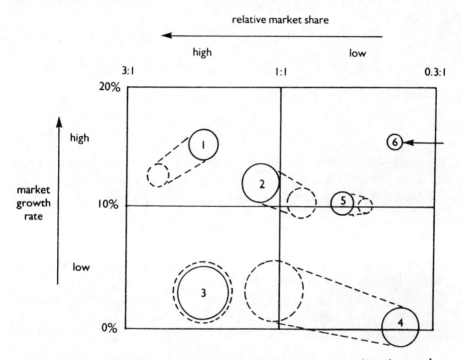

Figure 6.6 Example of portfolio matrix showing present situation and historical situation three years ago

Product 3 has changed very little in a stable market and the decrease in its percentage of overall company sales reflects an increase in overall sales rather than a decrease in the sales of that particular product. It is still very much a 'cash cow'.

Product 4 was a 'cash cow' but has now declined dramatically in a declining market. It has lost its market share, probably due to price-cutting by the competition.

Product 5 has grown faster than the market and has increased relative market share, albeit to a still relatively low share.

Product 6 did not exist three years ago and now accounts for 5 per cent of the company's sales volume.

From the development of these products over the last three

years, it is possible to suggest what will happen in the future without changed policies and how policies and strategies could be changed to achieve different objectives.

Objectives could be suggested from this portfolio matrix for individual products. For product 1 sensible objectives for a three-year plan could be:

- to increase sales by 30 per cent in real terms over the next three years

- to increase market share by 5 per cent over the next three years

For a one-year plan the objectives for product 1 could be:

- to increase sales by 10 per cent in real terms

- to increase market share by 2 per cent

As you can see, the objectives for year one are in line with the objectives for year three. Similarly, objectives could be suggested for some or all of the other products. Depending on whether the marketing plan was for one, some or all of the products, objectives would be added together to give an overall objective which could be:

- to increase sales by 8 per cent in real terms over three years

If the plan is only for one market or market segment, the Boston Matrix approach can be used for the company's products in that one market only and again conclusions can be drawn and objectives set.

For any company, the ideal product development sequence is to convert 'question marks' into 'stars' and for these 'stars' to ultimately become 'cash cows'. 'Cash cows' and unsuccessful 'question marks' will eventually become 'dogs'.

A company should aim for a balanced product portfolio with a reasonable number of 'cash cows' and 'stars' and not too many 'question marks' or 'dogs'. The ideal mix will depend on the company and the number of products in its portfolio. The surplus cash that is generated by the 'cash cows' is invested in the 'stars' and in a selected number of 'question marks'.

This analysis of the product portfolio will have direct implications for the objectives for these products in the marketing plan. A forecast matrix can now be produced showing where you expect the products to be at the end of the period of the marketing plan.

As well as being used to consider your product portfolio, the Boston Matrix approach can also be used to assess customers or market segments to decide which are the best areas for you to concentrate on. In this case the top of the matrix is your company/business strengths and the side of the matrix is the attractiveness of your key customers or market segments.

How to set achievable marketing objectives

Setting objectives for a marketing plan is not a simple and straightforward matter. Figures for sales turnover or market share cannot just be selected at random. It is an iterative process whereby objectives are set, strategies and action plans are developed, and then it is decided whether the planned objectives are impossible, achievable or easy. These objectives should then be reappraised and should they be changed, the strategies and action plans would also need to be re-examined. Marketing objectives should be difficult, but they must be achievable. The aim is to set objectives that are a challenge, but that can be achieved with effort. They must be motivating rather than discouraging.

In setting your objectives you should bear in mind the fact that if you have a large market share in a stable market, you are unlikely to be able to increase your market share dramatically. If a company is entering a new market and has only a 2 per cent market share, a 1 per cent increase in its share of the market represents a 50 per cent increase in its sales in that market. If a company already holds a 50 per cent share of a market, a 50 per cent increase in its sales would represent a 25 per cent increase in market share. This level of increase is usually impossible to achieve because as a company starts dramatically to increase its market share the competition tends to react.

Care should also be taken when defining a market. Many companies believe that they have a small market share in a large market, when in reality they actually have a large share of a much smaller segment of that market. For example, a supplier of industrial showers may have only a 5 per cent share of the total European market for showers, but may have 30 per cent of the more specialized market for supplying showers used in hazardous chemical areas.

Chapter 4 showed how historical sales figures should be presented for relevant products and relevant markets over the previous three years. It is important that historical sales figures should also be considered in absolute terms, ie with price increases removed, as was shown in Figure 4.5, or by numbers of units, as in Figure 4.6.

In forecasting, many companies base everything on an analysis of past sales. They take historical sales figures and project them forwards directly. The disadvantage with this method, if carried out in isolation, is that it assumes that what happened in the past will happen in the future and makes no allowance for changing conditions. A typical forecast based only on past sales would be as shown in Figure 6.7.

Sales forecasting is not that easy. Historical sales will rarely show a progression as smooth and regular as that shown in Figure 6.7. Figure 6.8 may be more typical of the graph of a company's sales growth.

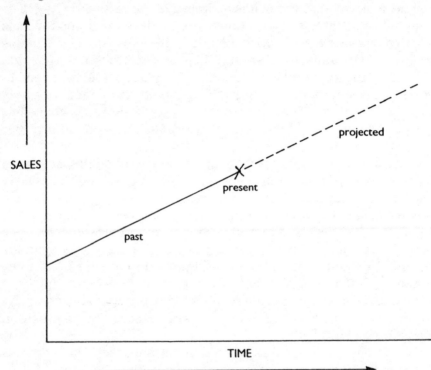

Figure 6.7 Typical sales projection based on past sales only

In looking at historical figures it is more realistic to look at sales rather than order figures. This is particularly the case if you have customers who place large orders for phased delivery over a long period of time. You should also consider whether in some years you have changed the date of implementation of price increases as this could also have a bearing on order intake levels and move some large orders forwards or backwards into another accounting year. This could account for some of the peaks and troughs on the sales growth curve.

With the type of curve shown in Figure 6.8, it is now not so easy to predict whether the product has reached its saturation stage and is about to decline or whether some of the fluctuations were due to changes in economic activity due to factors outside the company's control. You have to make a judgement on this based on the particular circumstances of your own product in your own market.

Figure 6.8 Irregular sales growth curve

How can projections for future sales be made more accurate?

The Boston Matrix approach allows you to make more reasoned judgements about sensible increases in sales, because to enter information in the matrix you need to predict not only your increase in sales in isolation, but also the change in your relative market share and the market growth rate. This means that you have to be able to predict how the market size will change.

Product/Market estimation

This technique helps you to build up a picture of the whole market for products of a particular type. Having estimated the total potential market, and knowing current market share, an estimate can be made of how the whole market will change in the future. An assessment can then be made of the effect the change in the size of the market will have on the product.

The types of factors that could be considered are increases/decreases in GNP, inflation rates, currency exchange rates, and commodity prices. It would normally be assumed that in times of recession, sales of products would decrease. In practice the reduction in sales levels would depend on the type of goods considered. When money is tight, it tends to be spent more on necessities than on luxuries.

It is actually possible to correlate quite accurately the likely effect on market size of changes in various economic indicators. Governments issue their own sets of forecasts based on the results coming from their own mathematical models, and various economic institutions such as banks and business schools do the same. These mathematical models are based on using statistical methods to show that the historical effects of various changes can be correlated and this correlation can then be projected forward to forecast future trends quite accurately.

Many large companies now prepare their own mathematical models. These models are normally computer based and, once set up, they can be used to predict different scenarios and are very useful in corporate and marketing planning.

At the marketing planning level, statistical methods can be used to see whether individual variables can be accurately correlated with investment potential or market size. Typically, the coefficient of correlation can be used to establish how close the relationship between the two variables is, and a regression analysis can then be carried out to predict future trends.

For example, for products used in the offshore oil industry, the total market would be influenced by changes in the price of oil and the exchange rate of the dollar compared with other major currencies. If the price of oil were rising, investment prospects in the industry would improve and the market for the products would probably also increase. The opposite would be true if the price of oil were falling.

A correlation could be made between the dollar price of oil and the level of investment anticipated. It could be that the level of investment in exploration in one year reflected the price of oil the previous year. Because of the longer time-scale for investment in oil production equipment, it could be that the level of investment in oil production would reflect the oil price three years previously.

Many companies can make quite simple correlations relating to their own industry. If interest and mortgage rates rise, it is likely that the number of new houses started in the following six months will reduce. If fewer new houses are being built there will be a reduction in the requirement for materials and components for houses. This will affect brickmakers and sanitaryware makers as well as paint and wallpaper manufacturers.

Individual product estimates

These are based on building up an individual estimate of what sales of the product could be over the period of the forecast. In the industrial goods sector it is an extension of the normal sales forecasting carried out by the sales organization and involves estimating what is likely to happen to sales to particular key customers and the effect that this will have on a product's total future sales. With many organizations this also involves asking distributors for an estimate of their likely purchases over the next year or even over the next three years. This information can be cross-checked using a stock-monitoring system, whereby distributors provide a regular list of their current stock levels for certain products. Sales can then be compared with stocks and current purchases and it is possible to predict whether an overstocking situation is likely to result in lower than expected orders in the future. Historical sales figures can also be reduced by an amount to compensate for distributor overstocking – this should give a more meaningful view of the true levels of past sales.

In the consumer goods field, microforecasting techniques are even more widespread and rely mainly on surveys of actual or potential customers. The techniques for carrying out these surveys were discussed in Chapter 3. From the individual customer level, a reasonably accurate figure for the likely total sales over a given period can be built up. This technique is only accurate over a short time period and cannot be realistically used to predict sales three or five years ahead.

Increasing performance

The techniques shown above will enable you to predict more accurately what future sales levels are likely to be with no change in your marketing strategies. But marketing and marketing planning are not just limited to predicting what will happen if nothing is changed; they also involve the setting of objectives and the implementation of strategies for increasing market share or moving into new markets.

Market potential curve

From the situation analysis, you have estimated your market share and those of your competitors. Using product/market estimation techniques, you can estimate the total potential market for your product. This is shown in Figure 6.9.

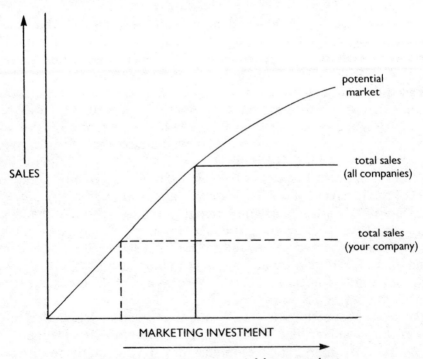

Figure 6.9 Marketing potential for a product

Your share of the market is influenced by the marketing investment in terms of advertising and sales promotion that your company puts into this product/market. An increase in this investment should increase sales. The effect will not, of course, be linear, because as you gain market share, your competitors are likely to react.

Gap analysis

Gap analysis is a technique which helps you to analyse and close the gap between what your company needs to achieve and what is likely to be achieved if policies are unchanged. It can be used to increase profits and also to increase sales turnover. It therefore follows that in a wider sense gap analysis can include suggestions for cutting costs, entering new markets, and for introducing or acquiring new products. We will consider it here from the point of view of setting objectives.

Figure 6.7 showed a sales forecast based on past trends and unchanged future policies. Companies are not satisfied with a situation where there is no real growth or low growth for a product. Even if a product is at the mature or saturation stage of its life cycle, it is still possible to increase sales by implementing various marketing techniques.

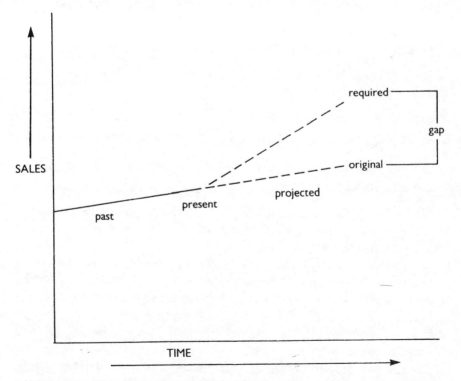

Figure 6.10 Revised sales forecast showing required and originally projected growth

Figure 6.10 shows a situation where the company requires a growth rate for the product that exceeds the growth rate projected from historical figures. The gap between the original and the required sales growth must not be so large that it is impossible, even with modified policies, to bridge it. So first you have to establish that the market potential is greater than the gap that you are trying to bridge.

You need to estimate the *TOTAL* potential market for your product. This, in effect, is the total market taken by all competing products in all markets as well as the potential for expansion into other sectors. You compare this figure with figures for your own sales into these markets and this determines the finite amount of expansion of sales that could theoretically be possible. Obviously you could never hope to achieve 100 per cent market penetration, but at least you now know what the outer limits are. The gap between your company sales and the total market potential is made up of a number of individual gaps:

- the gap taken by non-competing products in all markets

- the gap taken by competitors' products in existing markets

- the gap taken by competitors' products in geographical markets where you are not represented

- the gap taken by competitors' products in industry sectors where you are not represented

It therefore follows that this gap can be closed by:

- market penetration, ie increasing market share

- market extension, ie entering new geographical markets or entering new industry sectors

It can also be closed by entering new markets with new products, but since this is the most risky strategy, it is the least used if the other possibilities exist.

The use of gap analysis in setting marketing objectives is an iterative procedure. Consideration must be given to the strategies and the action plans that would need to be implemented in order to close the gap. It is only if it appears feasible to close the gap by such strategies that the objectives will be carried through into the final plan. If it seems that even with the strategies and proposed action plans, the gap is still too large to bridge, the objectives would need to be revised downwards and more realistic ones should be set. The preparation of strategies and action plans will be considered in the next chapter.

The presentation of the objectives

We have looked at ways of determining *achievable* objectives. This is the planning part of the process. The objectives also need to be presented in the written plan. First you should include a summary of your overall objectives. This would be a series of statements such as

- 'Increase sales of Product A in the UK in real terms by 5 per cent per annum over the next three years'

- 'Increase sales of Product B in Europe by 3 per cent per year in 19X3 and by 5 per cent per year in 19X4 and 19X5'

- 'Increase market share of Product C in USA to 10 per cent of market by 19X5'

You should then prepare detailed figures for your projections for sales, market share and profit, in accordance with the main objectives stated. With regard to sales figures, it is useful to show historical and projected figures in one table, so that the progression of sales can be easily seen. The presentation of these figures would therefore be an extension of the presentation of historical sales figures shown in Figures 4.1 and 4.2 in Chapter 4. An example is given in Figure 6.11.

SALES FIGURES						
SALES AREA: UK						
YEAR £/UNITS (delete as appropriate) PRODUCT A PRODUCT B PRODUCT C TOTAL	19X0	19X1	19X2	←— forecast —→ 19X3	19X4	19X5

Figure 6.11 Sales figures – historical and forecast

Another way of presenting the forecast figures for sales, market share and profit is shown in Figure 6.12. This has the advantage of showing sales, market share and gross profit together. Historical figures could also be included in the same table.

In a one-year plan a more detailed phased sales forecast would also be included; an example is shown in Figure 6.13.

MARKETING OBJECTIVES 19X3 – 19X5									
SALES AREA: UK									
£/UNITS (delete as appropriate)									
YEAR	19X3			19X4			19X5		
	Mkt Share %	Sales	Gross Profit %	Mkt Share %	Sales	Gross Profit %	Mkt Share %	Sales	Gross Profit %
PRODUCT A PRODUCT B PRODUCT C TOTAL									

Figure 6.12 Marketing objectives for three-year period

SALES FORECAST 19X3													
SALES AREA: UK													
£/UNITS (delete as appropriate)													
	J	F	M	A	M	J	J	A	S	O	N	D	TOTAL 19X3
PRODUCT A PRODUCT B PRODUCT C													
TOTAL SALES													

Figure 6.13 Sales forecast for a 12-month period

Summary

Setting marketing objectives is the key step in the preparation of a marketing plan. Marketing objectives are what we want to achieve with our plan; marketing strategies are how we get there.

Marketing objectives relate to any of the following:

- selling existing products into existing markets

- selling existing products into new markets

- selling new products into existing markets

- selling new products into new markets

Marketing objectives must be definable and quantifiable and should be expressed in terms of values or market shares.

All marketing plans should include objectives for:

- sales turnover for the period of the plan

- market share for the period of the plan

- gross profit on sales

Before setting your marketing objectives it is important to understand your present position with regard to products and markets. You should look at your product portfolio with regard to product life cycles and cash generation. The Boston Matrix is a useful tool for carrying out this analysis.

Although all forecasts are based on an analysis of past sales, they should also take into account the total potential market, the existing market share and the life cycle of the product.

Performance can be increased by considering the total potential market for your products and by using gap analysis to close the gap between what the company needs to achieve and what is likely to be achieved if policies are unchanged.

Marketing objectives ought to be difficult but achievable. The aim is to set objectives that are a challenge, but that can be achieved with effort. They must be motivating rather than discouraging.

7: Marketing Strategies, Tactics and Action Plans

Once the initial marketing objectives have been set, it is necessary to consider how they can be achieved. The way that you go about achieving your marketing objectives is through marketing strategies.

It is important to understand what strategy is and how it differs from tactics. *Strategies* are the broad methods chosen to achieve specific objectives. They describe the means of achieving the objectives in the time-scale required. They do not include the detail of the individual course of action that will be followed on a day-by-day or month-by-month basis: these are *tactics*. Strategy is the broad definition of how the objective is to be achieved, the action steps are tactics, and the action plans contain the detail of the individual actions, their timing, and who will carry them out.

The decision to 'market price' a product is therefore a strategy, but the decisions to decrease prices by a certain percentage in one market and to increase by a certain amount in another are tactics.

Marketing strategies are the means by which marketing objectives will be achieved. They relate to *products, pricing, advertising/promotion*, and *distribution*. They do of course also relate to selling, but selling is usually included under the heading of 'promotion'.

Marketing strategies relate to general policies for the following:

- Products
  - changing product portfolio/mix
  - dropping, adding or modifying products
  - changing design, quality or performance
  - consolidating/standardizing

- Price
  - changing price, terms or conditions for particular product groups in particular market segments
  - skimming policies
  - penetration policies
  - discount policies

- Promotion
  - changing selling/salesforce organization
  - changing advertising or sales promotion
  - changing public relations policy
  - increasing/decreasing exhibition coverage

- Distribution – changing channels
  – improving service

There will undoubtedly be many strategies that could be used and to include all of them in the plan would not be practical. It is, however, possible to narrow down the alternatives by considering only those strategies that offer the greatest chance of success. All of the strategies should be consistent with each other and with the objectives that they are expected to achieve. The strategies of the marketing plan should also be reconciled with those in the corporate or business plan. For example, if an objective in the corporate plan is to change company focus/direction, divest, specialize, retrench, hold/expand existing business, diversify, etc, this would need to be reflected in the proposed marketing plan.

Types of strategy

One way of looking at strategies is to consider whether they are defensive, developing or attacking. All strategies are one of these types or a combination of more than one

1. *Defensive strategies* – designed to prevent loss of existing customers.
In your SWOT analyses you will have listed a number of 'weaknesses'. These could relate to the company, its organization, the products or service offered. A number of strategies would be designed to overcome these weaknesses and to consolidate the company's position in the marketplace.
   If one weakness was that the company had a bad reputation for quality, the logical strategy would be 'to improve quality'. If the product was considered to be old-fashioned, the necessary strategy could be to repackage (for a consumer product) or re-engineer (for an industrial product).
   Typical defensive strategies would be:

- improve company image
- improve quality/reliability of product/service
- improve reliability of delivery promises
- restyle/repackage product/service
- improve performance of product
- improve durability of product

- overcome product faults

2. *Developing strategies* – designed to offer existing customers a wider range of your products or services

These strategies are based on modifying products or introducing new products to your existing customers in your existing markets. From your SWOT analyses, you will have identified a number of 'opportunities' that can be exploited. Some of these will relate to the market's requirements and how they are being fulfilled by your existing product or product range. If you have a range of four sizes of product, you may have identified a market requirement for another size of the product larger than your largest unit, or smaller than your smallest size. Examples of this are the introduction of bags of 'mini-bars' by chocolate companies, and paint in bulk size containers in DIY stores.

The introduction of such products can often offer the simplest and least risky strategy to increase turnover.

Typical developing strategies would be:

- increase range of sizes/colours/materials offered

- increase range of services offered

- increase range of extra features/options

- find different uses for product

- develop new product

- make product more environmentally friendly

3. *Attacking strategies* – designed to generate business through new customers

This type of strategy involves finding new customers for your product in your existing markets or new customers in new markets. No company has a 100 per cent coverage of its existing market and new customers can be found or attracted from competitors by offering better quality, price or service. Also, new customers can be found in new geographical or industry market segments.

Typical attacking strategies would be:

- change pricing policy

- use new sales channels

- find new distribution outlets

- enter new geographical markets

- enter new industry sectors

A useful way of looking at the types of strategy that may be available to a company is to use a matrix that was developed by Ansoff, as shown in Figure 7.1. It can be seen from this matrix that the least risky way to try to expand your business is in the areas that you know best – ie with your existing products in your existing markets.

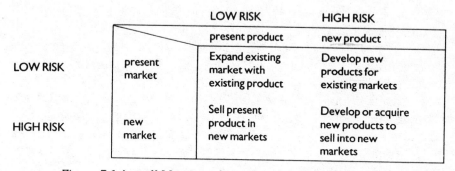

		LOW RISK	HIGH RISK
		present product	new product
LOW RISK	present market	Expand existing market with existing product	Develop new products for existing markets
HIGH RISK	new market	Sell present product in new markets	Develop or acquire new products to sell into new markets

Figure 7.1 Ansoff Matrix – the risks of various strategies

A higher risk strategy is to sell existing products into new markets, which involves the development of market entry strategies. At least with this type of strategy there is only one unknown – the new market – and you are selling something that you know you have sold successfully in your existing markets.

To develop new products for existing markets is an even more risky strategy, but one that most companies have to try at some time or another. If an existing product is reaching the end of its life cycle there will be no choice but to use a strategy of this type. Many companies have a continuing strategy of introducing one new product every few years to spread the risks.

To develop or acquire new products to sell into new markets is the most risky strategy of all and should not be attempted if other options are available.

Devising strategies

Strategies can come from many different sources and it is wise for a company to encourage its marketing executives to consider all possible ways of generating potential strategies. Some strategies may seem to follow logically and obviously from the objectives, but others may evolve in a flash of inspiration. It is a common practice in many companies to have 'brain-storming' sessions to devise a list of strategies. The same approach can also be used to consider possible tactics.

When the list of alternative strategies has been prepared, they should be evaluated to determine which will best satisfy the objectives. You should also determine which strategies can be best implemented with the resources and capabilities that your company has.

If a company only employs ten people and has a turnover of half a million pounds a year, then a strategy involving 'setting up a subsidiary company in France' would clearly be outside the resources and capabilities at its disposal, whereas in a much larger company with a multi-million-pound turnover this may be a logical strategy.

Strategies should be listed under the headings of the four main elements of the marketing mix – products, pricing, promotion and distribution. Examples of specific marketing strategies for these major functions are given below, together with some of the tactics that could be employed.

Products

STRATEGY: change product portfolio/mix
TACTICS:

- Offer only one product line
- Expand your product line to cover a wider market
- Develop separate products for different markets
- Make different versions of the product with different names for different markets
- Acquire new products that complement existing products through the acquisition of new companies

STRATEGY: drop, add or modify products
TACTICS:

- Drop marginal products
- Develop new products to supersede old products
- Launch modified product

STRATEGY: change design, quality or performance
TACTICS:

- Establish a quality image through the development of quality products

- Distinguish your product from your competitors' product in the eyes of your customers

- Establish a reputation for innovation

- Create new uses for your existing product by improving performance or by adding exclusive features

STRATEGY: consolidate/standardize the product
TACTICS:

- Rationalize your product line

- Drop expensive extras/specials

Pricing

STRATEGY: change price, terms or conditions for particular product groups in particular market segments
TACTICS:

- Price product low and obtain maximum profit on spare parts

- Price product high and use low mark-up on spare parts

- Use different prices and different price lists for different markets

- Devise strategy to meet specific pricing policies of competitors

- Set price at 10 per cent below market leader

- Reduce price of product to maximize sales (to allow increased production and reduce unit production cost)

STRATEGY: skimming policy
TACTICS:

- Set price of new product at a level 30 per cent above previous products

- Sell on new revolutionary design features and benefits

- Be prepared to reduce price as volume increases if competitors enter market

STRATEGY: penetration policy
TACTICS:

- Set low price for new product to discourage competitors from entering market

- Increase turnover to level where product becomes profitable at this price level

STRATEGY: discount policies
TACTICS:

- Offer quantity discount to encourage larger unit purchases

- Offer retrospective discount based on level of purchases this year

- Offer discount level for next year based on level of purchases this year

Advertising/Promotion

STRATEGY: change selling/salesforce organization
TACTICS:

- Strengthen sales organization

- Reorganize salesforce for particular area

- Introduce performance-related bonus scheme for salesforce

- Recruit additional sales personnel

- Increase sales effort for most profitable products

- Increase sales effort to increase sales to key/major customers

STRATEGY: change advertising/sales promotion
TACTICS:

- Increase advertising for the product in specific markets

- Start new advertising campaign

- Introduce voucher scheme

- Offer incentive scheme to distributors

- Carry out mail shot

- Increase company image advertising

- Carry out high key product launch

STRATEGY: increase exhibition coverage
TACTICS:

- Increase attendance and stand size at major industry exhibitions

- Use DTI assistance for overseas exhibitions

- Encourage overseas distributors to exhibit more and supply equipment and personnel as support

Distribution

STRATEGY: change channels
TACTICS:

- Set up own distribution direct to stores

- Change distributor for area

- Increase number of warehouses for product

- Reduce to use of only one large warehouse

STRATEGY: improve service
TACTICS:

- Set up national service network

- Arrange service through major company with service centres throughout the area.

The component plans

To prepare your marketing plan you have to be able to break down individual objectives and strategies into tactics and action plans. A key objective in the planning process is to satisfy yourself that the objectives that you have set are not just achievable but profitably achievable, and that the strategies adopted will allow these objectives to be achieved. It is the tactics and the action plans that will allow the plan to be implemented and these need to be decided and costed up. Once you have set your initial objectives and strategies, there are a number of different ways in which you can proceed.

You can divide your objectives into sub-objectives for your key products, strategic markets and key sales areas, or you can prepare sub-plans for 'products', 'price', 'promotion' and 'distribution'. In fact, you should adopt both approaches – the sub-objectives and strategies will ultimately be entered into the written plan under the sections 'key products, strategic markets and key sales areas' and the individual plans for the separate parts of the marketing mix will ensure that you are adopting a co-ordinated approach.

Sub-objectives

If your objective is 'to increase sales of the product by 10 per cent in real terms over two years', this objective will be broken down into a number of component parts. Some of the increase may come from an expected expansion of existing markets, but some will almost certainly be expected to come from expansion into new geographical or industry market segments.

A sub-objective could be 'to increase market share for the product in the German Market from 2 per cent to 10 per cent over two years'. Your strategies for this could be:

Product – Redesign the unit for the German market and in particular comply with DIN standards and carry out TUV testing as necessary.
Pricing – Set prices 10 per cent below price of market leader and hold this level for as long as necessary.
Promotion/Advertising – Hold training courses for German salespeople. Prepare and implement a major advertising campaign. Exhibit at major exhibitions such as the Hannover Fair and Achema Exhibition.
Distribution – Set up subsidiary company in Germany.

A sub-objective of a major confectionary manufacturer could be 'to introduce a new range of quality chocolates into the French market and achieve sales of 30 million francs per year within two years'. The strategies adopted could be:

Product – Redesign packaging for the French market to give an 'air of British quality and snob appeal', but use the French language, metric weights, etc.

Price – Price at similar levels to other high quality chocolates available in France.

Promotion/Advertising – Prepare and launch a quality advertising campaign on French TV and in up-market magazines. Get campaign organized by a major French advertising agency with a knowledge of the market.

Distribution – Distribute through up-market chain-stores, *confiseries*, etc.

The approach of individual plans involves looking at your overall approach to a particular part of the marketing mix.

The product plan

The preparation of the product plan involves looking at your product portfolio and deciding:

• if it should be changed

- how it should be changed
- what strategies you can adopt
- where these strategies will lead you

In Chapter 6 we looked at the historical and present position of the product portfolio, using the concept of the product life cycle and the Boston Matrix approach. In preparing the product plan we will use the information already gained from this and will develop it further.

The marketing decisions that we will take for a product will vary, depending on which quadrant of the Boston Matrix it is in. The different quadrants suggest different marketing responses.

Question mark – invest heavily in selected products that you believe have good growth potential
– consider dropping weak or risky products
Star – invest for growth
– improve competitive position
Cash cow – maintain your competitive market position
– manage the product to maximize earnings
Dog – minimize investment
– maximize cash flow short term
– consider dropping product

If we now look at the product portfolio from Chapter 6 as shown in Figure 6.6 (p. 107), we have the basis to make decisions about our current product range and where we can go with it.

Product 1 is still a star and sales have increased over the last three years. Nevertheless, the increase in sales has been slower than the growth rate of the market. There is therefore scope to make a higher investment in the future and to increase the growth of the product still further, even if there is some reduction in the market growth rate.

Product 2 has moved into the star sector and, again, greater investment will probably increase the sales of this product still further.

Product 3 will continue as a cash cow in a stable market, but its percentage of overall company sales will probably continue to decrease as the sales of the 'star' products continue to increase.

Product 4 is now very much a dog. Its demise is probably irreversible and further investment would not be worthwhile. In the lifetime of the marketing plan it will continue to reduce in sales turnover and become a prime target to be divested or dropped.

Product 5 has remained on the boundary between question mark and dog. A decision must be taken as to whether it will drop further into the 'dog' quadrant or whether it will move more towards the 'star' sector.

Product 6 did not exist three years ago and a more detailed analysis of its performance in each of the last two years would be necessary in order to decide which way this product is going. It is a new product and so no decision on its long-term future would be taken at this stage.

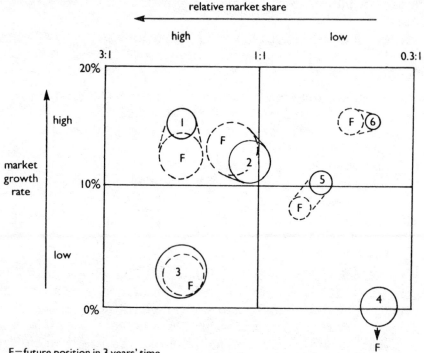

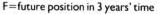

F=future position in 3 years' time

Figure 7.2 Example of portfolio matrix showing present position and projected position in three years' time

The typical scenario for this product portfolio in a three-year marketing plan is shown in Figure 7.2.

This portfolio matrix represents the company's objectives with regard to product, sales turnover and market share. The company would now adopt strategies with regard to price, promotion and distribution that would allow these objectives to be achieved.

The pricing plan

Pricing is a key factor in marketing strategy. It can be a major determinant of whether corporate and marketing objectives will be achieved. Its role needs to be established in relation to the product portfolio, the life cycles of the products, and the objectives for sales turnover and market share.

It is generally true to say that the price level of a product will determine the demand for that product. The price that you sell your product at, and the quantity that you sell, will determine the profit you will make from these sales.

If you reduce your price you would expect to increase the demand for your product. Figure 7.3 shows a typical demand curve.

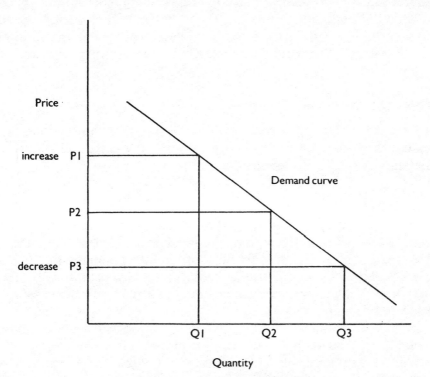

Figure 7.3 A typical demand curve

If you are currently selling your product at price P2 and you are selling a quantity Q2, the total value of sales is P2 × Q2. If you increase your price to P1, the quantity you sell will reduce to Q1 and if you decrease your price to P3 the quantity you sell will increase to Q3. The object of the exercise is to increase the value of sales P × Q to the maximum but to maintain P at a profitable level. If the cost of producing the items is above P3 you cannot justify reducing your price to P3 in the long term, because although you would sell more product it would be sold at a loss. There may, however, be good marketing reasons to justify reducing the price to P3 or below as a short-term measure to gain market share.

From an accounting point of view it makes no sense ever to sell a product at a loss. From a marketing point of view, however, you often have to consider the 'chicken and egg' situation. If the product is too highly priced, it may never sell in the quantities necessary for economies of scale to allow the product to be produced profitably. Japanese companies, in particular, have been prepared to sell products at the market price, rather than a price based upon initial cost. This has enabled them to build up market share quickly and then to make profits. Pricing must ultimately be related to costs, but cost is not the only factor that must be used to determine price in the marketing environment. The question of break-even quantities and costing is considered in more detail in Chapter 10.

Pricing strategies

There are many types of pricing strategies and tactics that can be considered. Most can, however, be broadly classified as either skimming policies or penetration policies.

Skimming

This involves entering the market at a high price level and 'skimming' off as much profit as possible. As competition enters the market, the price level would be adjusted downwards as necessary. This type of strategy can only be adopted by a company that has a clear lead over the competition. A company with a patented product that is way ahead of its competitors' products can successfully adopt a skimming policy.

This type of policy has typically been adopted by drug companies when they have such a lead. An example of this is Wellcome with its AIDS treatment drug. This is sold in the market at an extremely high price. There is, of course, the argument that such drugs cost huge sums of money to develop and that if the drug companies did not have the patent protection to enable them to adopt a skimming policy, they would not be able to generate the funds to invest in further development.

The problem with a skimming policy is that the high profits generated do encourage competitors to enter the market and to develop products that overcome your technological advantage. A skimming policy is also likely to keep the volume of product sold low (even though this is more than compensated for by the high profit level). This means that it is unlikely that the company will be able to benefit from economies of scale in manufacture.

Skimming policies, when feasible, are clearly advantageous to companies with new, innovative products where the costs of producing and marketing the product are known with any degree of accuracy.

Penetration

This is the opposite of skimming. With this type of strategy a company sets the price low deliberately. A penetration policy encourages more customers to purchase the product, which increases the company's sales turnover and also its market share. This in turn means that the company will be able to benefit from economies of scale in manufacture at an earlier stage than would otherwise be possible. Also, a low initial price may discourage competitors from investing in the development of competing products if the development costs are high.

A company operating a penetration policy may initially be selling the product at a loss on the basis that at that price it will rapidly achieve a level of turnover where the product will become profitable.

Penetration policies have been adopted by companies such as Sony in the US television market and Epson in the European computer printer market. Low market pricing has been combined with considerable marketing investment in both cases.

Premium pricing

Some products sell at a high price because of what they are or because of the reputation of the company that makes them. The selling price of Rolls Royce cars is higher than the average house price in England. Most people know this and if Rolls Royce tried to sell cars at the same price as Ford and General Motors, people would not believe that they really were Rolls Royces. The same holds true for Rolex watches. In fact, efforts by Mercedes to come down-market with the 190 Series and by General Motors to go up-market with the Senator were only partly successful.

There is the old story of the man in Piccadilly Circus trying to sell £10 notes for £5. He was unsuccessful, because everyone assumed that the notes were fakes. The concept of a quality product selling at a quality price is an important one. A price that is too low can be just as much of a disincentive to sales as a price that is too high. When Bulmers first introduced Babycham, it was a sparkling cider drink. It was a failure. It was later reintroduced at a much higher price as a 'champagne perry' and was a major success.

Differential market pricing

This is a tactic much used in marketing. It means that the price of the product will be varied in different markets, depending on the competitive situation. EU competition law makes it difficult to use such a tactic in Europe, but it may be that the price level for the product in the USA or Japan is much higher or lower than in the home market. The price for this market would be adjusted to allow penetration. If the business is marginal, it would justify selling at a lower price in some markets.

Companies also use specific market pricing against competitors who come into a market at a very low price to try to obtain market share. A market leader can, in some cases, prevent a competitor gaining a foothold in the market by market pricing where necessary, with specific customers and in specific areas.

Price leadership
The market leader is in a unique position. It is likely that other companies will set their prices based upon his price and will move prices after he moves – whether up or down. Because of his high market share the market leader is in a strong position to react to price changes from smaller competitors.

The life-cycle effect
The position of a product on its life-cycle curve or in a particular quadrant of the Boston Matrix will also determine the type of pricing strategy that is relevant. If a product is at the saturation stage of its life cycle and is also a 'cash cow' with a high and established market share it would be illogical to consider price cutting to try to increase market share. It would be far better to keep the price high for as long as possible to milk the product and to provide profits to support newer products. If, on the other hand, a product is at an early stage of its life cycle and is a 'question mark', it may well make sense to consider a penetration policy to increase market share.

Discounting
Pricing policy does not just relate to list prices. Discounting strategies are an integral part of the price equation. They are mainly relevant if you are selling through distribution channels, although even if you are selling directly to end-users, quantity discounts can be used. Discounts can be used to encourage larger individual orders or can be based upon the total amount of business placed in a given period of time. They can be used to encourage customers to buy from your company alone and not to spread the business between you and your competitors.

A company with a portfolio of products has an advantage over a single product company in terms of its pricing policies. It can gear the pricing strategies for particular products to the position of those products in their life cycles and the overall requirements of the company for profit. It can decide to forgo profit today on certain products in order to increase market share and to take its profits on other products that are more established in the marketplace.

With a portfolio of products it is possible to have a true pricing plan rather than just a collection of individual pricing strategies.

Further development of the individual plans for distribution and promotion will continue in the next chapter.

Action plans

Once you have selected the outline strategies and tactics to achieve your marketing objectives, you need to turn these strategies into programmes or action plans that will enable you to give clear instructions to your staff. Each department and each member of staff needs to know their responsibilities and the timetable for carrying them out, so each of your marketing strategies must have its action plan.

Each action plan should include:

• Current position – where you are now

• Aims – what to do/where you want to go

• Action – what you need to do to get there

• Person responsible – who will do it

• Start date

• Finish date

• Budgeted cost

If your marketing objective was 'to increase sales of the product in the UK by 5 per cent per year in real terms over the next three years', your strategies might include 'reorganize the salesforce in a more logical manner'. The action plan or programme for carrying out this strategy would include:

• Recruit sales manager by 1 June 19X0

• Define new sales areas by 1 September 19X0

• Set sales budgets for salespeople, territories, products, by 1 September 19X0

- Recruit additional sales engineers by 1 November 19X0

- Train new sales engineers by 1 January 19X1

The complete action plan would also include details of who would carry out the actions.

Each action plan would also need to be broken down into its component parts. Figure 7.4 shows a suggested layout for an action plan. This plan is to carry out the strategy of 'carry out a mail shot'.

ACTION PLAN						
DEPARTMENT: SALES						
Aim	Current Position	Action	By	Start	Finish	Cost
Carry out mail shot	Mailing list out of date	Update list	ILH	1.1.X1	1.3.X1	£200
	No standard letter	Prepare letter	JDT	1.2.X1	1.3.X1	£25
	No brochure	Prepare new brochure	NBF	1.11.X0	1.3.X1	£3,000
		Send out mail shot	ILH	1.3.X1	1.4.X1	£500

Figure 7.4 Presentation of an action plan

Each of the actions on this action plan could be broken down into a number of parts. In the preparation of the brochure there would be a number of stages, including:

- Having photographs taken

- Preparation of technical information by engineering department

- Preparation of preliminary layout

- Writing copy

- Preparation of artwork

- Final checking

- Printing

Each of these component parts would need to be detailed and the cost or the number of man hours required for each element estimated. A bar chart with week numbers on it should be prepared. An example for the brochure preparation is shown in Figure 7.5.

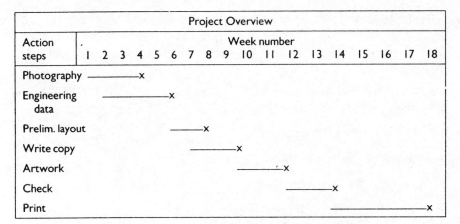

Project Overview																		
Action steps	Week number																	
	1	2	3	4	5	6	7	8	9	10	11	12	13	14	15	16	17	18
Photography ————x																		
Engineering data ————x																		
Prelim. layout ————x																		
Write copy ————x																		
Artwork ————x																		
Check ————x																		
Print ——————————x																		

Figure 7.5 Bar chart for brochure preparation

After scheduling your activities on the basis of action plans you should combine the individual action plans and programmes into the larger functional programmes (product, pricing, promotion, distribution). These functional programmes would appear in the written marketing plan. They would then be developed into an overall schedule – a master programme schedule that can be used for controlling the implementation of the plan. This is the 'schedule of what/where/how' in the written plan. Although it would only be the larger functional programmes and the master programme schedule that would appear in the written marketing plan, each of the smaller plans and programmes would need to be communicated to those who have to carry them out.

Summary

Marketing strategies are the methods by which you achieve your marketing objectives. They are the broad methods chosen and they describe the means of achieving the objectives in the time-scale required. The individual courses of action that are followed on a day-to-day basis are tactics.

Marketing strategies relate to *products, pricing, advertising/promotion* and *distribution*. They can be categorized as 'defensive', 'developing' or 'attacking' strategies.

As there will always be a huge range of potential strategies available to any company, those that will best satisfy your objectives and which can be effectively implemented using the resources and capabilities of your company should be selected.

Objectives should be divided into sub-objectives for your key products, strategic markets and key sales areas, and sub-plans should be prepared for 'products', 'price', 'promotion' and 'distribution'.

The product plan involves looking at your product portfolio and deciding:

• if it should be changed

• how it should be changed

• the strategies you can adopt

• where these strategies will lead you

The pricing plan determines pricing policy and tactics. It determines the mix of pricing and discount policies that best suits your product portfolio.

Strategies must be converted into programmes or action plans in order that they can be carried out. Each department and member of staff needs to know their responsibilities and the timetable for carrying them out.

These individual action plans are then combined into larger functional programmes which in turn are combined in the master programme schedule. It is the larger functional programmes and the master programme schedule which appear in the written marketing plan.

8: The Distribution, Advertising and Promotion Plans

Promotion means getting the right message to the right people. It involves personal selling, advertising and sales promotion. But before you can plan your advertising and sales promotion you need to select the right marketing channels for your product and your business from those available. This is part of the distribution plan. A distribution plan will always be part of a marketing plan, but in many companies, distribution is so important that there is also a separate distribution plan within the corporate plan (see Chapter 1, Figure 1.1).

The distribution plan

The physical distribution of goods is only one aspect of distribution as defined by marketing planners. Distribution involves:

- Marketing channels
- Physical distribution
- Customer service

Marketing channels

Marketing channels are the means that a company can select to get into contact with its potential customers. If its potential customers are unaware of the product, they will not buy it. There are a wide variety of different channels that a company can use. They vary from the impersonal to the face-to-face sale. Figure 8.1 shows a typical selection of available marketing channels.

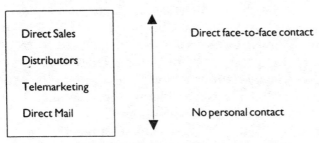

Figure 8.1 Marketing channels

Direct sales is an expensive channel to operate and is mainly restricted to high value industrial goods. (An exception is the door-to-door salesperson, although this technique is much less used now than it was ten or twenty years ago.) The bulk of advertising expenditure is used on consumer goods, particularly low value repeat buy items such as food and household consumables. Consumer goods are usually sold through distributors, wholesalers and retailers rather than through direct selling, but it is usually still necessary for the company to have a salesforce to sell to these distributors, wholesalers and retailers.

The characteristics of the product that you are selling will have a considerable influence on the mix of marketing channels that you finally select. Figure 8.2 shows how these product characteristics influence the choice between direct selling and distribution selling.

The number of levels of channels of distribution will also affect prices because of the level of discounts that will need to be built into the price structure.

A buyer buys to satisfy a need. That need consists of a mixture of objective and subjective parts. Objective needs are such things as the need to eat, the need to get from A to B, the need to manufacture an end-product at a certain cost in order to sell it in the marketplace. Subjective needs are emotional ones such as prestige or security. These are typified by such things as a wish to be seen to buy products which show you have wealth or are 'better than the Joneses'. In the UK, the rush to buy cars with the new registration letter in August is evidence of a mainly subjective desire.

The mix of objective and subjective needs will vary considerably from market to market. In the case of consumer goods the buyer is concerned largely with subjective needs such as emotional satisfaction, although he will also consider objective needs such as quality and price. An example is the 'own brand' consumer product marketed by large supermarkets. Unless the quality is similar to the quality of the branded product the consumer will not buy it even if it is cheaper. Luxury foods are purchased almost exclusively for emotional reasons. The same is true of luxury cars.

The industrial buyer will make his purchasing decision mainly on the basis of objective considerations – product performance, price, delivery, and the quality of manufacture. There will, however, also be subjective considerations such as the image of the product and the confidence that the buyer has in the company he or she is dealing with, and the salesperson himself.

Where products and prices are similar, subjective emotional considerations will decide which product is purchased. This choice

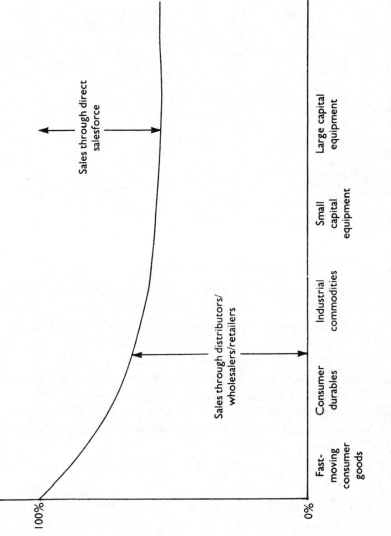

Figure 8.2 The influence of product characteristics on distribution channels

will be influenced considerably by the information that the company gives and the manner in which it is presented.

Figure 8.3 shows how objective and subjective needs influence purchasing decisions for consumer goods, industrial goods and services.

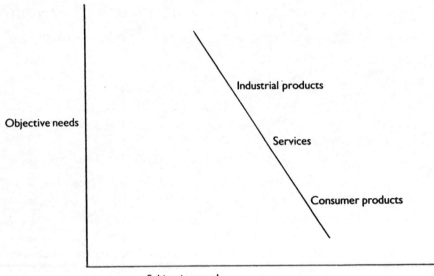

Figure 8.3 The effect of 'needs' on purchasing decisions

It follows that although personal contact selling can influence the client's subjective as well as objective considerations, it is more effective in industrial selling where objective considerations and technical understanding of the product have greater importance. The buyer of a fast sports car is more likely to have been influenced in his choice by the prestige of the product and media advertising than by the salesperson in the showroom who is only reinforcing the advertising message.

Direct Sales
In a perfect world direct selling with the salesperson face to face with the customer would give a company the maximum possibility of getting the message across and closing the sale. In the real world, this is not possible, because it is just not cost-effective. All companies employ a mixture of direct and indirect sales techniques.

The advantages of personal selling are:

• It allows two-way communication between the buyer and seller.

The buyer can ask questions about the product or service and the salesperson can provide information in response to these questions.

• The salesperson can tailor the presentation to the individual needs of the customer. The sales message is personalized.

• The salesperson comes to know and be known by the customers.

• The salesperson can negotiate directly on price, delivery, discounts.

• The salesperson can close the sale.

• The salesperson can monitor the customer response to the service received from the company in terms of delivery, quality, and after-sales service.

Distributors
In consumer goods industries distributors could be retailers, wholesalers or even companies that sell to wholesalers. In consumer markets it is usually the manufacturer who carries out the advertising campaigns to make the customer aware of the product. This is often the only way that the manufacturer can get his product message over to the customer. The wholesale/retail system means that the manufacturer can deal with a smaller number of accounts and make larger individual deliveries of products. Because wholesalers and retailers hold stock this reduces the manufacturer's requirement to do so. He also uses their knowledge of the market and customer contacts.

The manufacturer gives the wholesaler a trade discount. This is a discount from the price list. In most cases the discount is substantial because it has to cover the distributor's costs of stocking, buying in bulk, redistributing to retailers or end-users and, of course, his profit. So although the manufacturer saves the cost of direct selling, this is partially offset by the discount that he has to give to the distributor. There would also normally be quantity discounts that would be offered to distributors who order in large quantities.

The distribution channels available for consumer goods are shown in Figure 8.4.

For services the situation is different. There is no product on the shelf and so there is no requirement for wholesalers and retailers. The company supplying the service may sell it direct to the end-user or through an intermediary. The intermediary could be a commission agent, such as a travel agent or accommodation

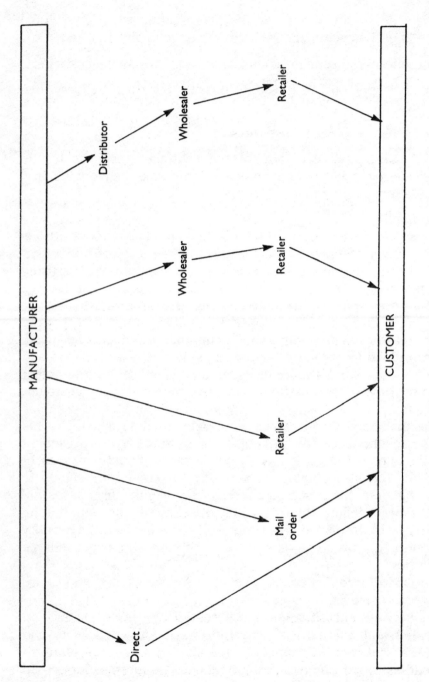

Figure 8.4 Distribution channels for consumer goods

bureau, or a franchise holder in the case of Dynarod (for cleaning drains) or many fast food chains. Figure 8.5 shows distribution channels for services.

For industrial goods it is not usual to use wholesale/retail outlets like those used for consumer goods. Direct sales to customers generally make up a larger proportion of sales than with consumer goods, but the use of commission agents and distributors is widespread. In the USA these commission agents are often called 'manufacturer's reps'. The most common distinction is that a distributor holds stock and an agent or rep does not. Figure 8.6 shows distribution channels for industrial goods.

Most industrial manufacturers have a direct salesforce. With industrial goods there will often be 'key accounts' who are serviced differently from smaller customers. Commission agents act on behalf of a number of manufacturers of different but related products. The order is normally placed on the manufacturer by the customer and a commission is paid to the agent. A distributor takes over the selling role of the manufacturer and most distributors will have their own salesforce dealing with customers. A distributor would normally be expected to hold enough stock to service the geographical area for which he is responsible. He may be an exclusive or non-exclusive distributor. In large geographical areas master distributors would have their own sub-distributors. In export markets, sales in conjunction with commission agents or through distributors are the most common methods. Most distributors sell a range of products, so a product will not get the exclusive treatment through a distributor's salesforce that it would through as company's own salesforce.

A direct salesforce can be structured:

- by product

- by area

- by account

Distributors can also be appointed on the same basis.

Telemarketing
Telemarketing is a relatively new sales method which is becoming increasingly popular as a supplement to salesforce activity. It involves selling and marketing by telephone rather than by direct physical contact. It originated in the USA and is used extensively there. It is easy to see the merits of telemarketing where distances between customers and between the manufacturer and customer

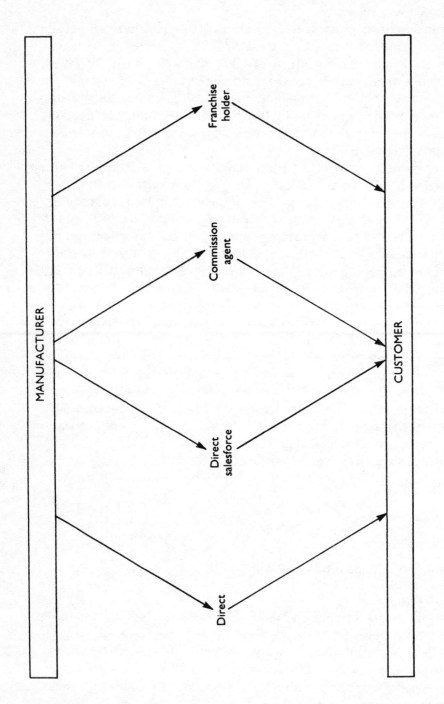

Figure 8.5 Distribution channels for services

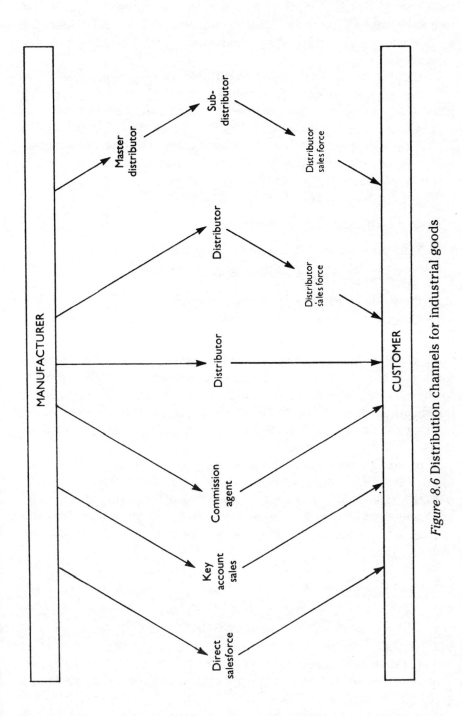

Figure 8.6 Distribution channels for industrial goods

are large and where the number of telephones installed is high. In areas of the USA and in Australia some companies now use telemarketing exclusively. As the number of telephones installed increases, telemarketing will gain ground in other developed countries as well.

Generally, it has been found that telemarketing is most effective when it supplements the field salesforce activity rather than completely replacing it. It is cost-effective because 40 to 50 telephone calls can be made per day whereas 6 to 10 personal visits per day is normal for direct sales calls. Internal sales staff have lower costs and related expenses than field sales personnel and this usually more than offsets the actual telephone costs.

The main advantages of telemarketing are:

• Lower cost than direct salesforce

• It frees up salesperson's time by reducing routine calling activity

• It increases frequency of customer contact

• It allows dormant accounts to be revived

Direct Mail
Direct mail includes mail order business and the use of mail shots. Mail shots involve sending information on a specific product by mail to potential customers on a mailing list. They are used more in the service and industrial goods industries than in the consumer goods industries. They rely for their success on the accuracy of the mailing list used, and a small return rate (as low as 2 per cent) is considered quite normal.

Mail order relies on customers placing orders by telephone or mail in response to advertisements or mail shots. It also involves ordering from mail order catalogues. The products that are ordered are then delivered either by mail or by a parcel carrier direct to the home. Mail order is almost exclusively used for consumer products.

Physical distribution

The cost of physically distributing goods is considerable. In many companies it accounts for as much as 20 per cent of the cost of the product. Whether your product is a chocolate bar, a car or an industrial cleaning system, it has to be delivered to the customer. This is an important part of the process of supplying products and getting them to the right place at the right time. It involves not only the transportation of the product and warehousing, but also the holding of stock, communicating within the distribution network and the way that the product is packaged for distribution.

Warehousing and factory location

The logistics of getting the product to market is an important factor in determining where a new factory will be built. The proximity to its main markets is important, as is the quality of the transport infrastructure. This is why the provision of good rail links to the channel tunnel is so important for British and French industry.

If your product is a high value industrial machine selling for tens of thousands of pounds, the siting of your factory is perhaps not so important as with lower value products. A few extra pounds on such a selling price is not particularly relevant. This makes feasible such projects as the Airbus, with production of different parts of the airbus aircraft in Britain, France, Germany, and Spain.

Logistics can involve the supply of raw materials as well as the finished product. This is why a European sugar factory will be situated near to the sugar beet fields and a pulp mill is normally sited near to the supply of wood necessary for its operation. It is usually more cost-effective to transport smaller quantities of higher value finished products over long distances than to transport large volumes of low value raw materials. The exception to this is where bulk delivery can be effected using large bulk carriers, as in the case of metal ores and crude oil.

The decisions relating to physical distribution that will normally be made in marketing planning relate to the mix of numbers of warehouses and transportation methods. This involves either increasing or decreasing the number of warehouses. For any organization there will be an optimum mix of warehouses and transportation methods. The warehousing may belong to your company, your distributors, or to both.

With the improvement in road transport links and the increase in lorry sizes in recent years many large companies with their own retail outlets such as DIY stores and major supermaket chains now find it more cost-effective to have only one or two central warehouses where all goods are received from suppliers, sorted, stored and then delivered by lorry direct to their big stores.

Companies that supply to a wide variety of outlets from large supermarket chains to little corner shops find it necessary to have a larger number of regional distribution warehouses and some deliveries may be made by smaller lorries or vans.

Stockholding

All companies want to have sufficient stocks of finished goods available to meet customer demand, but this has to be offset against the cost of holding stock. In times when interest rates are high, companies try to reduce stocks because of high interest charges. Finished goods need to be insured and there is always the risk that the stored product could deteriorate before it reaches the customer.

Transport

Companies have to decide on the most cost-effective way of transporting their goods. This involves deciding whether to purchase or lease their vehicle fleet or whether it is cheaper to use an outside transport company.

Communications

An effective communication system within the distribution network is necessary to avoid problems or mistakes in the processing of orders and in invoicing.

Packaging

The way that products are packaged for transportation can have a major impact on the cost of distribution. Decisions need to be taken relating to the size and shape of individual items and how they are packaged together or palleted, whether individual pallets can be stacked and whether the pallets are of the optimum size and shape for container transport.

Customer service

For the distribution plan we are only interested in the aspects of customer service that affect distribution. This really relates to the level of availability of the product to the customer.

Distribution is about getting the product to the right place (for the customer) at the right time. Theoretically you want to be able to offer your customers 100 per cent availability of the product. In practice there is no way that most companies can achieve this profitably. The difference in cost between offering a 90 per cent service and a 100 per cent service is probably a factor of at least 3 to 1 and yet the customer is unlikely to be able to tell the difference. The difference between a same-day service and a one-hour service will probably not be important to most customers, but would involve considerably higher costs to the company offering the latter service. It is necessary to find a balance between the costs and benefits involved in the customer service. The costs of extra availability should not exceed the extra revenue that will be gained as a result.

Putting together a distribution plan involves selecting your mix of marketing channels, deciding how to distribute the product, and setting a level of customer service that you want to achieve.

The two examples given below show the form that the final distribution plan might take for two different types of company. The first is a company selling chocolate bars (consumer) and the second is a company selling industrial valves (industrial).

1. The chocolate company

Marketing channels
The chocolate company will not consider telemarketing or direct mail as these are not applicable channels for this type of product. It will use a mix of direct sales (to the wholesale buyers) and distribution (distributors will sell to the small retailers). It will carry out nationwide advertising of the product to support these channels.

Physical distribution
The company manufactures this product in one factory only. It distributes the product by means of its own fleet of lorries to four regional warehouses. These warehouses hold one week's stock of the product, but these stocks are increased at times of traditional seasonal increased demand. Distribution to major wholesalers and distributors is also by means of its own fleet of lorries and deliveries are made twice-weekly. The company has an integrated live computer database showing stocks at all warehouses at all times. Orders from wholesalers are entered into the same database, order paperwork and invoices are transferred electronically to the warehouses and printed off on printers in these warehouses. The product is packed, 50 bars to a box, the boxes are packed 10 boxes to a larger box and these larger boxes are packed 10 to a pallet and shrink-wrapped on the pallet.

Customer service
Deliveries are made twice-weekly to major wholesalers.

2. The industrial valve company

Marketing channels
The industrial valve company uses a mixture of direct sales (to large key accounts and contracting companies) and distributors (who hold stock of valves and spares and service the market).

It has recently started to use telemarketing to follow up dormant accounts.

Physical distribution

The company manufactures all valves at its factory in Scotland and holds a stock of components and spare parts at the factory. It does not stock finished valves and only supplies to order. The company's distributors operate on a discount level of 30 per cent, from the company's list price and this finances the stocks of valves and spares that they hold. The company has two vans but these are not used to deliver product to customers. Deliveries are made using local haulage contractors. More urgent deliveries are made using nationwide overnight services such as TNT Overnite or Securicor or British Rail Red Star. The company operates an MRP (Materials Resource Planning) system with a computer database that includes order processing and invoicing. In addition the company operates a computer database for its distribution network and can advise one distributor where he can find a component (with another distributor) if he does not have it in stock. The valves are supplied shrink-wrapped in a rectangular polystyrene pack which is labelled with details of its size and materials of construction. Spares are supplied as 'spares kits' which are again shrink-wrapped.

Customer service

Customers are referred to their nearest distributor and the customer database for the distribution network will tell the distributor where he can obtain a component if he does not have it in stock himself.

The advertising promotions plan

As we have indicated, your advertising and promotions plan involves personnel, advertising and promotions.

Personnel

Once you have selected your mix of distribution channels you can decide on the personnel requirements of your plan. If you are intending to sell everywhere through a direct salesforce, you will need more sales personnel than if all your sales are through distributors. Even if all of your sales are through distributors you will still need regional sales managers to look after the distributors' accounts.

Your product will determine to some extent the channels that you use. If you were selling power stations worth £500 million each, you would use your own salesforce and local agents where necessary, because no-one is going to stock power stations and there is no such thing as a power station spare part! Spares would relate to individual items in the power station itself.

If you were selling industrial clips with a value of less than one pound per item you would not be selling directly to your customers. You would be selling your product to stocking distributors who would sell to the end-users.

In the situation analysis you will have carried out a SWOT analysis for your sales organization. This will indicate weaknesses that need to be addressed. You need to detail your existing sales structure and the proposed structure for your plan. You also need to indicate which of your personnel are existing and which will be additional.

It may be that you will not need any additional staff to carry out your plan: your existing resources may be adequate. You may not need to restructure your sales and marketing organization. This is important. Extra staff are expensive and restructuring can be disruptive in the short term. You should examine your personnel resources and how they are structured and only propose changes that are really necessary.

Your organization may be correctly structured, but coverage in certain areas may be weak. If your plan involves increasing export sales from a low level, you will almost certainly need to consider increasing export sales staff. If you intend to enter a new industry as a major part of your plan, it is likely that you will need to recruit a person with knowledge of that industry.

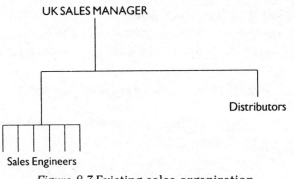

Figure 8.7 Existing sales organization

In our example we consider a company selling control valves. Its traditional market has been in the chemical and petrochemical industries. It sells direct to end-users with its direct salesforce and also sells through distributors who stock the product for resale. It has sold in this way for many years. The existing sales organization is shown in Figure 8.7. It has recently started to make significant inroads into the water industry, which is a new industry totally different to its traditional markets. As part of its marketing plan it is proposed to change its sales structure to that shown in Figure 8.8. This involves the appointment of a product/sales manager for the new market (water treatment) and a distributor sales manager to manage and extend the distributor network.

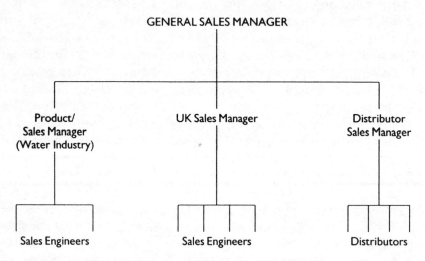

Figure 8.8 Proposed new sales organization

From this the company would then produce a list of existing and additional sales personnel as shown in Table 8.1. The cost of the extra three employees would be included in the budget and income statement in a later part of the plan. This is considered in Chapter 10.

Table 8.1 New and existing sales personnel

Position	Existing Personnel	New Personnel	Total
General Sales Mgr		1	1
UK Sales Mgr	1		1
Distributor Sales Mgr		1	1
Water Industry Sales Mgr		1	1
Sales Engineers	6		6
Total	7	3	10

Advertising

The purpose of advertising is to get a message across to the customer. Advertising operates at three levels – it informs, persuades and reinforces in the following ways:

It informs potential customers about the company and its products. This is the creation of awareness.

- It advises customers of the benefits of the products and tells them why they should buy these products rather than other ones. It creates the desire to buy or own the product. This is the stage of persuasion.

- It reinforces existing positive attitudes in existing customers

Advertising to inform normally relates to the promotion of new products and services. Advertising to persuade and reinforce is what most people understand as advertising. There is also the public relations side of advertising – promotional public relations. This includes media relations and exhibitions.

Media relations is an important part of the advertising plan. It involves the cost of lobbying and liaising, but these costs are low compared with the costs of purchasing advertising space. When using the media to gain attention for the company, its products and services, it is important to remember that the media are not working for the company, they are working for their own viewers, listeners, subscribers or readers. You cannot therefore assume that if you place large amounts of advertising with magazines, journals or newspapers, you will automatically get editorial coverage of your products. Most editorials, whether as an item on the BBC's *Tomorrow's World* or in a magazine, will only cover new, revolutionary products. The product has to be newsworthy.

Nevertheless, many companies do gain considerable publicity for themselves and their products by promotional public relations using press releases to pass information about new products and services, or improvements in existing products, to specialized publications dealing with their industry. In fact, there are many trade or specialized publications that need to provide background articles on products and companies supplying their industry. They are often only too pleased to receive approaches from companies prepared to put such articles together.

The use of exhibitions is another means of making the company and its products known to its potential customers. The cost of exhibitions can be high and tends to be higher for large companies who need to take a large stand to promote the 'right image'. Smaller companies can take small stands without it appearing that they are cutting costs or penny-pinching. Most companies limit the number of exhibitions they take part in and with new exhibitions appearing every year, it is often difficult to decide which exhibitions will be worthwhile. Many companies now only exhibit in the major exhibitions relating to their industry. However, although an exhibition can be an excellent place to launch a new product, it does make the competition immediately aware of your plans. For this reason many product launches now take place either in hotels or at the company itself, with a select invited audience of potential major clients.

Direct advertising is expensive and must be used as an integral part of the whole marketing effort. It needs to be targeted effectively. There is no point in advertising a local carwash on national television. This is obvious, but there are many pitfalls that are not so obvious.

Because advertising on television and in the national press is very expensive, most television and national press advertising relates to consumer goods with large annual sales, or services such as banking and insurance from large companies. Where industrial advertising does take place in these media it is mainly corporate image advertising for large companies such as BP, Shell and ICI.

Consumer goods companies can easily get marketing information relating their products (or equivalent products) to the types of people that buy them. In Chapter 3 we discussed classification systems such as PIN and ACORN. Companies selling advertising space also provide details of reader or viewer breakdown. Table 8.2 shows the breakdown of national daily newspaper readership in PIN neighbourhoods from a recent *National Readership Survey*.

The logic of advertising Rolls Royce cars in the quality newspapers rather than the popular press can clearly be seen from this readership survey. Similar survey information on the age breakdown of readers would indicate which newspapers are best for advertising investment schemes for the over 65s or mortgage deals for the under 25s.

The advertising of industrial or capital goods uses much narrower and more specific outlets than the advertising of fast-moving consumer goods or consumer durables. The products are generally aimed at a much smaller number of end-users and advertising will normally be placed in industry-specific technical magazines.

A company selling equipment used in food production would advertise in magazines such as *Food Manufacture*; a company selling equipment used in the pulp and paper industry would advertise in *PPI (Pulp and Paper International)*. Each industry and each industry sector has its own technical press and their advertising departments can normally provide details of circulation by number, area, and type of reader (plant manager, engineer, management, etc).

Table 8.2 Readership of national daily newspapers based on PIN neighbourhood types

	D	L	K
Qualities			
The Daily Telegraph	236	24	62
The Times	216	28	58
The Guardian	152	49	198
The Independent	191	41	85
The Financial Times	244	31	126
Middle			
Daily Express	134	64	66
Daily Mail	148	46	57
Today	116	86	100
Populars			
The Daily Mirror	56	133	125
The Sun	62	116	120
The Star	40	153	141

(Average readership for all PIN areas = 100)
Key: D = Affluent neighbourhoods
    L = Crowded council housing
    K = Poor multiethnic areas

Objectives for your advertising have to be set up and these objectives must be realistic. You need to define both the audience that you wish to reach and why you need to reach them. A company that says 'we never know how successful our advertising is' is not planning or monitoring its advertising correctly and may be throwing money down the drain. You cannot measure the success of your advertising directly in sales, but there are many techniques for measuring the effectiveness of a campaign.

In consumer goods industries the effect of advertising is often measured by carrying out consumer surveys. With industrial goods it is a matter of noting the number of responses or 'reader replies' from each advertisement in the technical press.

For your advertising campaign you need to answer the following questions:

• Who are the target audience?

• What is your message?

- What response do you want to get from the target audience?
- How can you best get this response?
- What is the most cost-effective medium for your advertising?
- When should you advertise?
- How long should the advertising campaign be?
- How are you going to measure the results?
- How much money are you going to spend?

You need to tie in your advertising objectives with your marketing objectives. If you feel that you need to spend £50,000 on advertising as one of your strategies to meet a specific marketing objective, but have only been allocated £30,000, you will either have to consider other strategies to help you to achieve your marketing objective, or change that objective.

It is important to spend money on advertising in a logical way. If you are selling industrial equipment and you are budgeting to spend £10,000 on a campaign, you would not spend it in a few minutes' television advertising or a one-page advertisement in a major national newspaper. You would spend it over a six- to twelve-months period by advertising in a range of trade journals/magazines. The same advert repeated every week or every month in a limited number of outlets is more effective than different one-off adverts in a wide range of outlets.

The example given in Figure 8.9 is the schedule for an advertising campaign that an industrial manufacturer selling equipment used in the water treatment industry might adopt.

PRESS ADVERTISING																
Product: controllers										Year: 19×1						
Media	No	Rate per insertion £	Total cost £	J	F	M	A	M	J	J	A	S	O	N	D
Water & Waste Treatment	4	800	3,200	×			×			×		×			
Water Services	4	750	3,000		×			×			×		×		
Water Bulletin	6	400	2,400	×	×	×		×		×		×		×	
IWPC Yearbook	1	900	900	×											
Total cost			9,500												

Figure 8.9 Press advertising schedule

Care would be taken in deciding which editions of various magazines to use. The editorial programmes of magazines are normally known for the whole year. These would have been checked and where possible, the advertisements would be tied in when magazines were carrying features on similar products (in this case instrumentation or control equipment). The company would attempt to get editorial space for its product as well.

A company selling consumer products such as chocolate or breakfast cereal would normally have a much wider spread of advertising coverage, but it would still be a co-ordinated campaign. Care would be taken to get the best mix of TV, poster, and press advertising. If you consider that Mars sell 2 million Mars bars in the UK *every day* and Rowntrees sell 4 million Kit Kats you can appreciate that advertising budgets for such products are likely to be several million pounds a year.

Sales promotions

Sales promotion covers more or less everything that you can do to give customers a tangible incentive to purchase your product. In the UK sales promotion usually means some special offer, either to the customer or the salesperson, to help to promote sales. It is widely used for consumer goods and the amount spent on sales promotion in the UK is estimated to be in excess of £5 billion, making it similar in size to expenditure on advertising.

The spectacular growth in the use of sales promotion dates from the late 1960s and sales promotion expenditure in real terms in many markets has grown fivefold in that time. This reflects a change in western economies, from 'pull' purchasing to 'push' selling. With the spread of supermarkets, hypermarkets and self-service outlets, there are now a huge number of brands of almost everything competing for the same consumer. More inducement is necessary to get people to buy a particular product.

A sales promotion must have the following elements:

• it must be a featured offer and not part of normal trade

• the offer must give the customer some tangible advantage

• it must be designed to achieve an increase in sales over a specific time period

A sales promotion will normally contain one of the following catchwords – 'free', 'save' or 'win'.

A sales promotion cannot take the place of advertising or selling and it cannot change long-term trends in the life of a product or brand. It can, however, encourage a consumer to behave more in line with the economic interests of the manufacturer. It can:

- increase volume sales in the short term

- stimulate stock movement

- encourage repeat purchase

- increase customer awareness/loyalty/purchase frequency

- increase market penetration of new product

- bring forward buying peaks

- dispose of old models before a new model is introduced

In the consumer goods industries, the most common forms of sales promotions are such things as vouchers giving '10 pence off your next purchase of the product', 'three for the price of two' or 'an extra 10 per cent volume for the same price'. Other schemes provide items such as free video cassettes, crockery or kitchen equipment if you send a certain number of wrappers (showing proof of purchase) plus a nominal amount to cover postage and packing. Petrol companies are well known for their giveaways in petrol sales promotion schemes.

Manufacturers also run sales promotion schemes for their staff where the prize is something like a holiday for two for the sales-person or distributor of the year. It is becoming more common now for companies to relate a certain part of the salaries of their sales personnel to performance against budget. It is also common for manufacturers to carry out limited duration sales promotions during which their own sales personnel or their distributors' sales personnel receive a certain value in vouchers redeemable at stores such as Argos, Boots, or Marks & Spencer for every sale of a specific machine that they achieve during the period of the promotion.

Specific promotions can be a good way of gaining additional sales for specific products. It is amazing how hard people will work or what they are prepared to do to get 'something for nothing'.

Sales promotions are often badly managed and regarded as just another advertising or general marketing expense. In fact, a sales promotion needs to increase the contribution to the company from the sales of that product. If a product makes a contribution of £1, a sales promotion offering 10p off your next purchase needs to bring about a 10 per cent increase in sales just to make the same contribution. An increase of more than 10 per cent is necessary for the promotion to start to be successful.

In the same way that you need to set objectives for advertising campaigns, you also need to set your objectives for sales promotions. Objectives for sales promotions could be:

- to increase sales by X per cent

- to introduce a new product

- to encourage repeat purchases

- to combat competition

- to move buying peaks

- to increase sales out of season

To be effective a sales promotion must have a well defined but limited timespan. If your product is always offered at a 10 per cent discount this will eventually become the market price.

A typical sales promotion campaign for a manufacturer of ice cream based frozen deserts could be as follows:

Objective: To stimulate sales of 'Arctic Delight' throughout the months of January, February and March when sales are traditionally low because of cold weather. It is expected that the promotion will increase the value of goods sold by 10 per cent and that there will also be additional advantages to the company. It will be able to:

- continue production at normal rates

- reduce stock costs (low temperature storage)

- improve cash flow

The promotion will involve the sale of 'Arctic Delight' in new, special packaging. The packs have a voucher on them, and this can be traded in for a 20p reduction (10 per cent) in the price of further packs of 'Arctic Delight' (only one voucher per pack) until the end of the offer. To promote the offer, the company will request stores to stock more 'Arctic Delight' and in return it will provide free of charge special display boards and promotional posters. The company will also carry out a press and TV advertising campaign to support the promotion.

In preparing your marketing plan, the details of each of your individual advertising and sales promotion campaigns will be included in your action plans. The total costs for each campaign need to be included in the advertising and promotions plan together with the cost of promotional public relations and exhibitions. There should be an overall advertising and promotions schedule and additional schedules showing expenditure for each part of the advertising and sales promotion campaigns.

Advertising and Promotions Schedule for 19×1						
Advertising	Type	TV	Press	Poster	In store	Comments
Big Bar	Launch	×	×	×		All campaigns to coincide and start 1 April
Promotions						
Big Bar	Launch				×	2p off next purchase Duration 3 months from 1 June
Exhibitions						
Big Bar	Interchoc					Launch to trade in February

Figure 8.10 Advertising and promotions schedule for new large chocolate bar

EXHIBITION COSTS	
Name of exhibition: Interchoc Location: NEC (Birmingham) Date: 14th-18th February 19x1 Stand size: 100 m²(10m x 10m) Stand contractor: Bunyon & Baynes	
Costs	£
Stand space rental	5,000
Design, supply and build	25,000
Artwork, photographic panels	5,000
Rental of carpets furniture, lights, phone, etc	3,000
Hotel bills/expenses for stand staff	5,000
TOTALS	43,000

Figure 8.11 Schedule of expenditure for Interchoc exhibition

Figure 8.10 shows the type of advertising and promotions plan that might be included in the marketing plan for a new chocolate bar by a chocolate company.

There would be an additional schedule showing the expenditure for each part of the advertising and promotion campaigns. The schedule of expenditure for exhibitions is shown in Figure 8.11.

Summary

Implementing a marketing plan requires communication, which means getting the right message over to the right people. This involves personal selling, advertising and sales promotion.

Before you can put together your advertising and promotions plan, you need to select the right marketing channels for your product and your business from those available. This is part of the distribution plan and you will need to decide the mix of direct sales and distribution through distributors, wholesalers, retailers, etc. The characteristics of the product will influence the mix of channels used.

As well as the selection of marketing channels, the distribution plan also includes the physical distribution of goods and customer service.

Once the distribution plan is complete, advertising and sales promotion can be planned and personnel requirements can be decided. The advertising and promotions plan should include details of the present structure of your sales organization and any changes proposed for the implementation of the marketing plan.

Advertising informs, persuades and reinforces ideas about products. As well as pure advertising, it includes promotional public relations activities such as media relations and exhibitions. It is expensive and must be used as an integral part of the whole marketing effort. It needs to be targeted effectively and the results must be monitored.

The same is true of sales promotions. These are special offers either to the customer or to the salesperson to help to promote sales of a specific product.

The advertising and promotions plan should include the details, schedules and costs of the advertising and sales promotion campaigns that are included in the marketing plan.

9: Sales Areas – Different Approaches for Different Markets

Not all products are the same, and different areas or countries require different approaches.

Basic types of products

From a marketing point of view there are three basic types of products. These are

- Consumer goods
- Industrial goods
- Services

There are, of course, some products that could be in all three categories. Paint is an example. It can be purchased by both consumers and industrial companies and it can also be part of the 'service offering' given by a house decorating company. It is also true that not all industrial goods are capital goods and that some consumer goods such as houses or cars are capital items to the purchaser. Nevertheless, these broad definitions hold in most cases and key marketing principles apply equally to the marketing of consumer goods, capital goods and services. It is just the way that the principles are applied that takes a different form.

Consumer goods

Consumer markets are characterized by having a large number of customers. By their very nature consumer goods are usually items that are mass produced in identical form.

There are two basic types of consumer goods: fast-moving consumer goods and consumer durables.

Fast-moving consumer goods – *sometimes called convenience goods* These are items such as foods, tobacco, drinks and cosmetics that have a quick turnover and tend to be quickly consumed.

Consumer durables   – These are items such as cars, fur-
niture, clothing and electrical goods
which are less frequent purchases that
will be used by the customer for a
long time.

The consumer is normally taken to be the end-user who may or may
not be the actual customer who purchases the goods. A consumer
may purchase a television set. A chocolate bar could be purchased
by a mother to be consumed by her children or for consumption
by herself.

Within the consumer goods industry different marketing techniques have been developed for fast-moving consumer goods and
for consumer durables. For example, a car manufacturer may wish
to convey to the customer the fact that its make of car will not
rust for seven years, but a chocolate manufacturer would not want
customers to remember that its chocolate bars have a shelf-life of
seven years. The chocolate manufacturer wants the customer to
remember such things as the taste of the bar, the size, and the fact
that it doesn't melt in your hand. The car manufacturer wants the
customer to remember such things as shape, speed and reliability.

Until recently most books on marketing, market research and
marketing planning concentrated on the consumer goods industries.
Because of the size of consumer markets, consumer data is the most
widely collected and analysed type of information available.

Most consumer markets are segmented – ie there are markets
within markets. Consumers can be classified by characteristics
such as their age, sex, socio-economic group or occupation. These
characteristics will have a bearing on the type of television programmes they will watch and the newspapers they will read. Since
it is expensive to advertise and sell on a national scale, it is important
for companies to know which type of customer is likely to buy their
product and to target their advertising accordingly. A company
selling Rolls Royce cars is more likely to advertise in *The Times*
than in the *Sun* newspaper. Equally, a company selling skate-boards
is unlikely to advertise in the *Financial Times* !.

In the consumer goods field it is easy to find out what types of
customer are likely to buy a particular type of product and to find
out what type of advertising is most likely to reach these customers
by using market research techniques of the types shown in Chapter
3. The supply chain for consumer goods is often quite long. Figure
9.1 shows the supply chain for a breakfast cereal. The bulk of the
advertising would be aimed at the customer and the consumer.

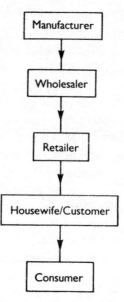

Figure 9.1 Supply chain for breakfast cereal

Industrial goods

Industrial goods are any goods sold by industrial companies to manufacturers, suppliers, contractors or government agencies. The goods would normally be incorporated into other products, used within the company's own business, or resold.

Industrial goods can be raw materials, components or capital goods. The ultimate consumer of the final product probably has little interest in the raw materials or components used in its manufacture. These would include the valves and pipework in a soap manufacturing plant as well as the chemicals used in soap manufacture.

The same principles of marketing apply to industrial goods as apply to consumer goods. It is, however, much more difficult to apply these principles in industrial markets, because information about industrial markets is not so easily available as that about consumer markets. This is because industrial markets are more specific. There will only be a limited number of potential customers for ball-bearings and they will probably be different from the potential customers for industrial showers. Companies within these fields would therefore have to commission market research individually. In consumer goods marketing, the customers who buy chocolate bars would be the same customers who buy soap powder, so that the same market research information could be of use to companies selling both of these products. The demand for industrial goods ultimately derives from the demand for consumer goods, because the users of industrial goods are usually the manufacturers of consumer goods. Although the connections between the two are complex, nevertheless if sales of dairy products were booming, the industrial companies supplying equipment to the dairy industry would expect their sales to increase as well.

It is a fact that the marketing of industrial goods and *particularly the marketing of capital goods* is more difficult than the marketing of other types of products, because there are fewer individual customers and each industrial market has its own specific characteristics.

One hundred years ago, there were few manufacturers of industrial goods and the products almost sold themselves. There are still many companies selling industrial goods who mistakenly believe that well engineered quality products will sell themselves. That may have been true 100 years ago but it is no longer the case. There is now fierce international competition and all products – including industrial goods – need to be marketed effectively.

Twenty-five years ago, in his book *Marketing Management*, G.B. Giles stated:

'While there has been a movement on the part of some manufacturers in the consumer goods area to woo the end-consumer – the housewife, there has been almost no effort at all on the part of the manufacturers of capital equipment and industrial material which are produced for use by other manufacturers to discover the needs of the customer. It is not unusual to find top executives in these industries afraid that their customers might think of them as a selling organization.'

There are still unfortunately too many companies even today with the philosophy 'You cannot sell machinery in the same way as soap'. Although the detail would be different, the steps in the preparation of a marketing plan would be similar whether your product was soap or machinery.

The supply chain in the sale of capital goods is shorter than the supply chain in selling consumer goods and the number of individual customers for the product is considerably less.

Capital goods are often sold directly to the end-user – this is almost never the case with consumer goods which are usually sold through complex distribution networks. A supplier of chocolate bars could have 30 million final customers, whereas a company supplying capital goods is unlikely to have more than a few thousand customers for its products.

Figure 9.2 shows the supply chain for a manufacturer of capital equipment who supplies components to other companies who build machines, and also complete machines to companies who use these machines to manufacture their products.

Because of the diversity and complexity of markets for industrial goods, there is not as much outside expertise as in the consumer sector and companies need to rely heavily on their own employees for market information or interpretation of outside information. In the industrial sector the number of key players and competitors in any particular industry is usually small.

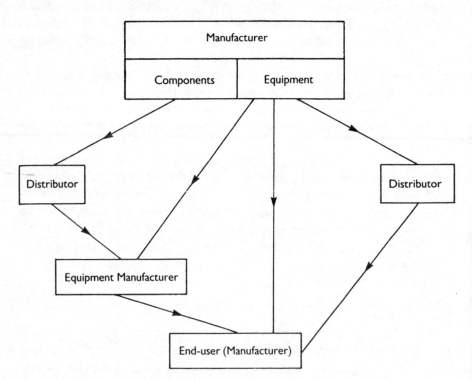

Figure 9.2 Supply chain for capital equipment supplier

Services

The third basic type of product is a service. By this we do not mean the customer service that most reputable companies supply with their products, but a service as a product in its own right.

Services range from financial services such as banking and

insurance to cleaning windows and carrying out electrical repairs. They differ from consumer and industrial goods in that in a service industry there is no tangible product and the product has no shelf-life. This is an important fact, which influences the way in which services are marketed.

In a service company many of the functional activities are different to those in a manufacturing company. As there is no 'product' there is no need for warehousing, distribution or quality control functions. There is also no need for engineering, research and development, purchasing or production departments. Since the 'product' is being sold, a service company must still have finance, operations, sales and marketing functions.

Since the product has no shelf-life, a service organization must be able to get continuity of work. Because there is no actual product the advertising used to promote services is different from that used with consumer or industrial goods. Service organizations sell the benefits of their service as their product.

You cannot fail to notice that in any set of *Yellow Pages* there will be more entries for services than for manufacturers. This is because manufacturers often have more cost-effective methods of advertising. Most services are by their very nature local and the *Yellow Pages* is the 'buyer's guide' to local services.

In a service organization your marketing needs to at least produce enough sales at the right margins to ensure survival and preferably it should produce better sales to facilitate profits and growth. You need to maximize the volume and quality of customer contacts, by attracting more, converting more, satisfying more and making better contacts. The means of achieving this are:

- Improve contacts with existing customers

- Improve contacts with known potential customers who do not use your services

- Identify and make contact with new potential customers

Because a service is not a tangible product it is easy for your potential customers to be confused as to what you are really offering. You therefore need to consider – *what your service really is*. How does this compare with:

- What you currently think your service is?

- What your buyers know your service is?

- What your non-buyers think or know your service to be?

As an example, consider a photographic company offering a '24-hour film processing service'. If the company does not have the resources always to actually provide this service at peak times of the year there will be different perceptions of the service that they are offering.

The company thinks that it is offering a 24-hour film processing service. It is actually offering a 24- to 48-hour processing service. Its non-customers know from experience that it cannot guarantee 24-hour service, and its customers are prepared to put up with this.

Success in the service sector is dependent on your image and reputation. Advertising, direct mail and personal contact are therefore all-important.

In your marketing planning you should also bear in mind that it is your total profit and profit margin that is important rather than your turnover. This is true in all industries, but it is particularly important in service industries. Large industrial manufacturing companies have large overheads to be recovered and even marginal business which shows no profit can at least recover overheads. Although there are exceptions, such as hotel chains and airlines which have high overheads, many service companies are relatively small with low overheads and their labour costs make up a large part of their total costs. You should consider ways of turning away marginal business and maximizing more profitable business.

Approaches for selected markets

Just as basic marketing principles need to be adapted to the differences between consumer goods, industrial goods, and services, consideration needs to be given also to regional and geographical differences. It is not possible to give detailed information on all geographical markets, but the following notes give some guidelines on the major industrial markets.

Some differences are obvious – more chocolate is sold in cold and temperate countries than in hot countries, and more ice cream is sold in hot countries than in cold countries. Other differences are not so obvious: those between various regions of the same country are not usually as marked as those between different countries.

In marketing planning it is important to consider the suitability of a product for a particular type of market.

Simple agricultural tools may find a ready market in developing and developed countries alike, but sophisticated capital equipment

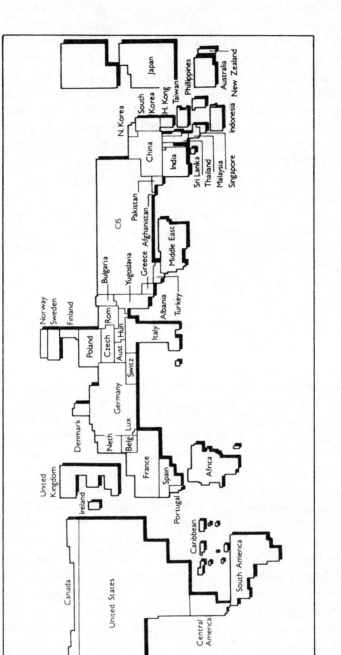

Figure 9.3 The distribution of world GNP (country sizes in proportion to GNP)

Source: *Financial Times* 26 September 1989, based on an original cartogram in *The New State of the World Atlas* by M Kidron and R Segal.

is more likely to find a market in developed countries. Even though luxury goods will be sold in developing countries, the size of the market for them will be proportionately larger in the richer, industrialized countries.

The measure of a country's wealth is its gross national or gross domestic product (GNP or GDP). Figure 9.3 shows a map of the economic world with the size of each country represented by its GNP. This economic map bears no resemblance to the geographical map of the world. It may come as a surprise to find that the GNP of the United Kingdom is about as big as the GNP of the whole of Africa or that the GNP of Germany is bigger than the GNP of the whole of South America.

When you consider selling to export markets, it is important to consider the cost-effectiveness of building up sales in one market rather than another. You need very good reasons for developing the African or South American markets before you develop your sales in Western Europe or the USA.

The European Union (EU) and other trading blocs

The UK does more trade now with Europe than with any other trading bloc.

There are three major trading blocs in the world who together account for nearly three-quarters of world trade. These are North America (USA/Nafta), Asia Pacific (Japan/Asean) and the European Union (EU). Half of the world's trade takes place within the EU. Even the external trade of the EU is greater than the external trade of the USA and Japan combined. Its population is larger than that of the USA and its combined gross national product is larger than that of Japan or the USA. Figure 9.4 shows comparative data for the EU, Nafta, and Asia Pacific.

The EEC was founded in 1957 when the Treaty of Rome was signed by West Germany, France, Italy, Holland, Belgium and Luxembourg. These countries were joined by the UK, Ireland and Denmark in 1973, Greece in 1981, Spain and Portugal in 1986 and Austria, Finland and Sweden in 1995.

In 1991 in Maastricht EC leaders agreed on the texts of a Treaty on European Union, Economic and Monetary Union (EMU) and associated protocols. The EU came into force in November 1993 and, subject to various criteria being met, it is intended that economic and monetary union with a single currency will be introduced by 1 January 1999.

There are now 15 separate countries in the EU ranging from

Luxembourg with a population of less than half a million to Germany with its population of more than 80 million.

	EU	Nafta	Asia Pacific
Population (millions)	380	370	1670
GDP (billion $)	6800	6700	4800
Car Sales (millions)	11.5	9.5	7.0
Exports outside own bloc (billion $)	565	400	360

Figure 9.4 Comparative data for major trading blocs (1993)

With the creation of the single market in 1992 and the expansion into the EU in 1995, the EU is now the 'home market' for every company operating within it. Companies based in England can sell directly to customers in Rome or Frankfurt and French companies can bid for refuse collection contracts in London. There are still some obstacles, but there is now an ever-increasing move towards European rather than national standards throughout the EU.

The North American Free Trade Agreement (NAFTA) was ratified in 1993, but it is far less far-ranging than the EU treaties. It is an agreement to gradually eliminate almost all trade and investment restrictions between the USA, Canada and Mexico over 15 years. Whereas the EU is a single market, NAFTA is far less integrated. Workers cannot move freely between NAFTA countries; members of NAFTA still, unlike EU countries, take anti-dumping actions against each other; and USA, Canada and Mexico set their own tariffs, while there is a common tariff on imports to the EU.

The Asia Pacific grouping is even looser and whereas the EU and NAFTA are based on treaties, in Asia, economic integration is based on market forces. Chief among these forces is the region's hothouse growth averaging more than 6 per cent per year.

Although there is talk of widening free trade areas between NAFTA and the EU, the real trend is towards regionalization of trade with rapid growth forecast in intra-regional trade. Many companies are responding to this trend by regionalizing their sales and marketing approach into the three areas of the Americas, Europe and Asia Pacific.

Germany

Germany has the largest economy in Europe. It has a very wide industrial base, so it is extremely unlikely that you will not encounter any local competition. Its trading practices are open and there is therefore competition from all over the world.

Although there are a number of specific 'industrial areas', such as the Ruhr, where heavy industry tends to predominate, you will find quite large industrial concerns all over Germany in towns and villages as well as in the big cities. It is quite common to find a factory almost in the middle of nowhere in a small village. There are still a large number of family-owned businesses in Germany. This is the case even with some very large organizations.

Germany is a federal republic consisting of 16 *Länder* or states. The distribution system reflects both the size and the federal structure of the country. Agents or distributors covering the whole country are rare, and most are still regional – with the bulk of their business in either the north or the south. They may insist that they can cover the whole of Germany, but unless they have at least three or four branch offices they will not give you effective coverage. Typical distribution would be based in Hamburg, Düsseldorf, Frankfurt, Stuttgart, Munich and Berlin.

In development terms, the old 'East' is many years behind the west and in spite of massive investment, it will be the turn of the century before it really catches up. You cannot expect distribution in the east to be as comprehensive or sophisticated as in the west, but in the long-term the opportunities are just as great.

For most products, the German market is at least twice as large as the UK market. There is also considerable potential to sell components to German companies that are exporting equipment or plant. In particular Germany is very strong in mechanical engineering and the export of industrial plant. These exports have traditionally been strong in Eastern Europe and as these economies transform and recover, this will continue. Although you can do substantial business in Germany through distributors, if you want to become a major player in the German market you need your own company there. This can be achieved by setting up your own company or by acquisition of a German company.

Acquisition is undoubtedly the quickest route if you can find a suitable company for sale. Because of the nature of the German company sector, with many concerns family-owned, this can often be difficult.

The Germans have a well deserved reputation for efficiency and quality. To get into the German market you must be good at what you do and to stay there you must be able to stay ahead technically. You must be prepared to meet buyers' requirements in design, price, delivery and standards and your literature must be available in German.

In business the Germans tend to be formal (particularly in the south of the country) and people who have been working together for twenty years will still refer to each other as 'Herr Schmidt' or 'Doktor Schmidt'. You should do the same. Although things are changing with the younger generation, the American style of using christian names at first meetings is not acceptable in Germany.

France

France is the largest country in Western Europe. Twenty per cent of the population live in Paris, which has assumed an economic and commercial importance greater than that of any other city in France. Paris is the centre of industry, banking, insurance and foreign trade. Most French companies of any size have an office in Paris, whether or not this is the head office. But if your product is to be sold all over France your distributor should have branch offices in cities such as Lyons, Marseille, Bordeaux and Nantes. Otherwise you should consider appointing local agents or distributors in the regions. It is often the case that although a company has an office in Paris, the main factory is out in the provinces.

France has nearly 30 per cent of the EU's usable farmland and agriculture is a major industry, occupying about 8 per cent of the working population and contributing some 6 per cent of GNP. French industrial development since 1945 has tended to favour the consumer goods industries and vehicle production. France also has well developed defence and nuclear industries. Nevertheless, it suffers (in the same way as the UK) from a narrow industrial base. This means that although in many industries there is stiff local competition, there are many gaps that offer potential to companies with the right type and quality of product.

A knowledge of the French language is essential if you want to do business in France. This knowledge can come from French speaking members of your staff or from English speaking members of the staff of your distributor or company in France.

Most companies start by appointing an agent or distributor and then progress to setting up their own sales office when the volume of business justifies it.

There are regional differences between Paris, the west and the south of the country and business tends to be conducted in a more formal manner in Paris than in the provinces. In business the French tend to be distant rather than formal. They may not be punctual themselves, but they will expect you to be punctual. If you are late for an appointment you will be received coolly – if at all. It is true that you will be expected to shake hands at the start and end of meetings, but this is just a habit. It takes a long time to build up personal relationships when conducting business in France.

Italy

The GNP of Italy now equals or exceeds that of the UK and the importance of this market should not be underestimated.

Although Rome is the official capital of Italy, Milan is the commercial capital. Industry is concentrated in the large cities of the north of the country and the south is predominantly agricultural. A distributor or local company should therefore be set up in the north where most industry is situated.

Engineering, construction and textiles are Italy's three biggest industries. Fiat is Europe's biggest car maker and Olivetti is Europe's major producer of personal computers. Italian industry is well known at home and abroad for the design and style of their products.

The Italians are less formal than the Germans and less distant than the French. They are very conscious of their level and status within their company and titles are very important. They can be volatile in temperament, but are always charming – even when saying no. They are well known for their lack of punctuality and it is wise to check by telephone beforehand that your arranged meeting is still scheduled to take place. The Italians love to haggle – especially over price and are not well known for prompt payment. Nevertheless there are plenty of business opportunities in Italy and perseverance pays dividends in the long run.

Other European countries

None of the other European countries, with the possible exception of Russia, can compare with the UK, Germany, France and Italy in population and industrial size. The most common way of selling into the smaller countries is therefore through a local distributor. There is much French influence in Belgium. Holland and the Scandinavian countries have their own individual styles with which the British and the Germans are familiar. The Scandinavians in particular buy and sell high quality, state-of-the-art products. The cost of doing business in these countries reflects the high cost and standard of living that their citizens enjoy. The old eastern countries such as Poland, Hungary and the Czech Republic are developing into market economies. The changes have been painful and difficult, but there are good opportunities in the longer term.

USA

The USA is the world's largest economy and the GNP of just one state – California – would rank it in the top ten nations of the world if it were a separate country. As the US market is so large in itself, many companies can make a perfectly good living without ever getting involved in exporting. Many American companies are only active in one state or one area of the USA.

In a country where individual states are often larger than several European countries, distance is a problem. You cannot set up a company in New Jersey and assume that this company will be able to sell your product throughout the USA. Any company is only as good as its distribution network and it is quite common for a company to be 'big' on the East Coast but unknown on the West Coast. If you choose to sell in the USA through a local company, you will probably find that this restricts your business to the geographical areas where this company is strong.

Because the key to success in the USA is distribution, many companies set up their own company to run their distribution network. I am not suggesting that your own company will do any better at putting salesmen on the road to cover a wider area than a distributor, but it will be able to plan on a nationwide basis. You can appoint regional managers for various areas of the USA (anywhere from 2 to 12 regional managers is common). These regional managers would be responsible for appointing distributors and representatives in major cities in their region. You could end up with more than a hundred distributors countrywide and these distributor accounts would be handled by your regional managers.

Distributors in the USA tend to be successful in specific industries such as aerospace, chemicals, pulp and paper, or water treatment. If your product is sold into two completely different industries you would probably have to run two completely separate sets of distributors for these industries.

The costs of setting up in the USA are high and the costs of running a nationwide organization are not inconsiderable, but the rewards are also high if you are successful.

With the advent of NAFTA, there is now also the possibility of setting up a manufacturing unit in low cost Mexico to manufacture your product for the American market.

Japan

Japan's per capita income has overtaken that of the USA. Its economy is second only to the US economy in size and could well overtake it early in the next century. In recent years Japan has been moving out of the old smokestack industries and into higher technology industries. This is a trend which has been accelerating with the dramatic appreciation of the yen over the last ten years. Japan is the world's largest manufacturer of motor vehicles and is a major force in semiconductors, electronic goods, machine tools and industrial robots.

Tokyo is the commercial and financial centre of Japan. The headquarters of most Japanese corporations are in the greater Tokyo area. The bulk of Japanese industry and population is situated in the coastal plain from Tokyo to Osaka.

The pace of doing business in Japan is much slower than in the USA or Europe. Much store is placed on personal relationships and doing things in the proper manner. Unless you have visited Japan it is difficult to understand how totally different it is to any other country in the world. For three hundred years until 1868 Japan was completely isolated from the outside world. In that time they developed different solutions to many problems and these solutions were often different to the solutions adopted in the outside world. Over the last hundred years the Japanese have modernized by keeping the best of the old and incorporating the best of the new from outside.

If you want to do business with Japan you need to understand Japanese business etiquette. There are many books dealing with this complex subject and you should read one before starting to deal with the Japanese. In Japan 'Face' is all important. The Japanese language is very complicated and it takes at least a year of full time study to achieve a reasonable conversational ability. The Japanese will be extremely pleased if a foreigner makes an attempt to learn a few simple words, but attempts to use a limited knowledge of the language for business conversation will normally be counterproductive. Interpreters should be used in all business dealings.

It follows that you cannot just get onto a plane and set off to do business in Japan. The Exports to Japan Unit (EJU) of the DTI can provide initial advice to UK exporters entering the Japanese market. Also the Japan External Trade Organization (JETRO) has offices in most major industrialized countries to help promote imports to Japan.

The recent appreciation of the yen has made western industry much more competitive in the Japanese market. There are still barriers to doing business in Japan, but these are coming down all the time. The biggest barrier is the complex distribution system and this is a problem to new Japanese companies as well as to exporters to Japan. To do anything in Japan you need a local presence – whether this is a distributor or a local company. The most common way of dealing with Japan is to find a distributor and as business grows, to consider setting up a joint venture company.

Many companies have been surprised at how quickly they have made progress in the Japanese market in recent years.

China and Asia Pacific

Make no mistake about it, the development of manufacturing and trade is moving firmly eastwards – and that does not just mean Japan. A recent report by the Australian National University predicts that by the year 2005, China will be the world's second largest economy, in the top half-dozen trading economies, and the largest trading partner of each of its neighbours.

Hong Kong and Singapore have already crossed the threshold from developing to developed nation status. Taiwan and South Korea are not so far behind. In western countries a growth rate of 4 per cent per year is considered good, in Asia Pacific a growth rate of 6 per cent per year is considered average and 10 per cent is good.

For western companies the main difficulty is to decide where to start. After Japan there is no clear choice, but the newly industrialized economies of Hong Kong, Singapore, South Korea and Taiwan are the most logical. Hong Kong can be used as a springboard to China and it is the overseas Chinese who are pushing much of the development in the region.

Although there are some common traits such as the Chinese work ethic, family ties, Buddhism and Confucian values, it is important to understand that each of these countries is individual with its own history and culture.

Kogan Page publishes an excellent series of books entitled *Sales Success in Asia: Dealing with Customers in . . .* which will give the reader guidance in doing business in nine key Asian countries.

Summary

There are three basic types of products: consumer goods, industrial goods, and services. There may also be an element of service in consumer or industrial goods. Although key marketing principles apply to all of these types of products, they are applied differently.

Consumer markets are characterized by being large markets with a large number of individual customers. Because of the size of the markets, consumer data is widely collected and analysed and readily available.

Industrial goods are normally sold to companies that incorporate them into other products, use them in their business, or resell them. Information about industrial markets is not so easily available as consumer information, because industrial markets are more specific, with fewer individual customers.

Services differ from other types of product in that there is no tangible product to sell and the product has no shelf-life. Service organizations sell the benefits of their service as their product.

Just as basic marketing principles need to be adapted to the differences between consumer goods, industrial goods and services, regional and geographical differences must be catered for. Consideration should be given to the size and importance of different geographical markets. The European Union, North America and Asia Pacific are the major trading blocs accounting for nearly three-quarters of world trade between them.

10: Budgets and Income Statements

In carrying out the marketing planning process and preparing your plan, you have already seen how to decide on strategies and to prepare the action plans to enable you to carry out your strategies and achieve your objectives. You have seen how realistic objectives can be set. But what about your strategies and action plans? They may be feasible, but are they cost-effective? If the cost of implementing your strategies and carrying out your action plans is greater than the contribution to company profits resulting from the additional sales forecast in the plan, you might as well forget the plan now – unless you can devise other strategies to achieve the same objectives.

How can you decide if your marketing plan is worthwhile? This is the most difficult part of the whole process and it is not uncommon to see marketing plans with objectives, strategies and action plans without any costs or any attempt to evaluate the cost-effectiveness of what is being proposed.

In this chapter we will look at budgeting and what techniques can be used to decide whether particular courses of action are cost-effective.

There are many analogies between the overall budgeting process and the marketing planning process. Both involve planning, measuring and controlling future activities. Before we look in detail at the way to cost up and evaluate your plan we must look in more detail at the overall process of budgeting and some of the accounting terms and methods used in this process.

The budgeting process

When a company prepares its budgets, there are three main stages to the overall process:

• The setting of financial objectives

• Budgetary planning

• Budgetary control

First, objectives are set. These would be the company objectives for the budgeted period (normally one year) and would relate to such things as growth, profit, and return on capital. These objectives are then translated into budget plans. The process is shown in Figure 10.1.

Once the board of directors have decided on the overall financial objectives for the company, the annual budget can be prepared. Until the forecast order intake has been agreed, other departments cannot proceed with the preparation of their budget plans. The forecast order intake will determine the forecast level of invoiced sales and this in turn will determine the amount of labour and materials that the company will utilize. Overhead recovery rates can be set and the individual budget plans can be gradually assembled until the overall company budget is complete. This sounds straightforward, but in practice the initial sums rarely balance and the process is iterative with adjustments to turnover, product mix and expense budgets until the overall company objectives are met.

The company budgeting process produces the budget used in the company business plan and when it is put into operation, it is used to control the company's activities. It must be monitored on a regular basis and if necessary corrective action can be taken.

The projected sales income, sales expenses and the cost of the additional sales will have an impact on the company profit and loss account and it is important that you understand what a profit and loss account is.

Profit and loss account

The profit and loss account is a summary of the success or failure of the transactions of a company over a period of time. It lists income generated and costs incurred. A typical profit and loss account is shown in Figure 10.2.

From the point of view of our marketing plan, we are not interested in anything below the line of operating profit, because our marketing activities will only affect items reported above this line in the profit and loss account. A detailed analysis of the whole profit and loss account and other aspects of company accounts is outside the scope of this book, but it is important to understand some of the key items reported.

Turnover
The turnover represents the total amount of revenue earned during the year from the company's normal trading operations.

Cost of sales
This represents the direct costs of making the product that is sold. The costs are primarily labour and materials.

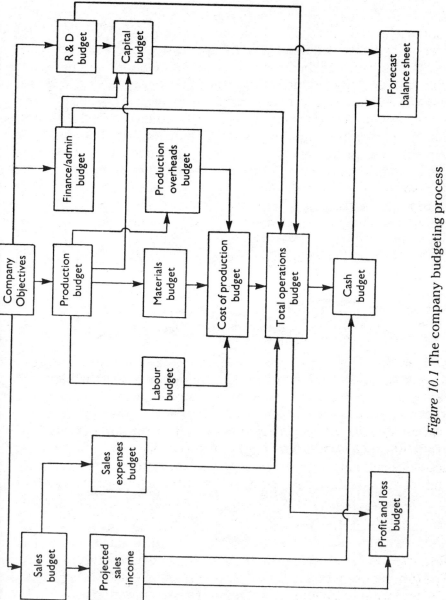

Figure 10.1 The company budgeting process

		£000
Turnover		6,000
less Cost of Sales		4,000
Gross Profit		2,000
less Distribution Costs	100	
Operating Expenses	800	
		900
Operating Profit		1,100
Income from Investments	50	
less Interest Payable	100	
		50
Net profit before tax		1,050
Tax on ordinary activities		500
Profit on ordinary activities after tax		550
Profit for financial year		550
Dividends		350
Transfer to reserves		200

Figure 10.2 Typical company profit and loss account

Gross profit

When the cost of sales is removed from the turnover, the resultant figure is the gross profit. This gives a direct comparison between what the product can be sold for and what it costs to make. This 'margin' has to be sufficient to cover all of the other costs and overheads incurred in running the business.

Other costs

These would include distribution costs, administration and operating expenses. This includes the cost of running the sales and marketing department together with advertising and promotional costs. It would also include head office salaries, rates, electricity, depreciation and the cost of research and development.

Operating profit

This is the key figure in the accounts as far as we are concerned. It is the net result of trading for the year, when total sales revenue is compared with the expenses incurred in earning that revenue. It is the ultimate measure of whether it has been worthwhile staying in business.

Budgeting the cost of a marketing plan

Your marketing plan is a part of the company business plan, whether it is a plan for your marketing activities for a single product, single market or for all of your products in all of your markets. It is the responsibility of the sales and marketing director to collate all of the separate marketing plans into the overall company marketing plan. We must therefore consider not only how to prepare the sales budget for the overall company marketing plan, but also how to cost up individual marketing plans and to calculate their effect on the overall company business plan.

Figure 10.1 showed the whole company budgeting process. In budgeting and evaluating marketing plans we only need to consider a part of this whole process. Figure 10.3 shows the part that is most important in evaluating marketing plans.

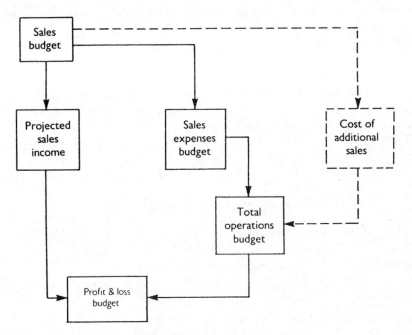

Figure 10.3 Budgeting for additional sales

It is only if your product is a new one or if you are forecasting considerable increases in business from your plan that capital investment may also be required.

It is clear that your marketing plan – whether for a single product or for all of your products – will include forecast figures for turnover and operating expenses. In Chapter 7 we considered how to decide on strategies and prepare and cost out action plans. The cost of these action plans should be included in the forecast operating expenses.

There is a difference in the way that budgeting is carried out for the overall company marketing plan and for marketing plans for individual products, markets or new products.

The overall company marketing plan

Budgeting of the overall company marketing plan is part of the overall budgeting process for the company budget that is included in the business plan, and needs to be carried out by the sales and marketing department in conjunction with other departments in the company. It requires the preparation of the sales budget first, because expenditure cannot be planned until the source and amount of income has been estimated. The sales budget consists of two parts – the projected sales income and the selling expenses budget.

Projected sales income

The forecast sales volume has been estimated earlier in the preparation of the plan based on the size of the market, forecast growth, the selling prices of the products and the impact of competition. It constitutes one of the key objectives of the marketing plan. The sales and marketing department will be working to forecasts of order intake and these must be converted to forecasts of unit sales and invoiced sales to be of any use to the production and finance departments in the preparation of their budgets. The phasing of the budget over the course of the year is also important. Figures 10.4 and 10.5 show the sales forecast and sales budget for a small manufacturer of colour televisions, VCRs and video cameras.

		SALES FORECAST 19×1				
PRODUCT	UNIT PRICE	QUARTER				TOTAL
		1	2	3	4	
	£	UNITS	UNITS	UNITS	UNITS	UNITS
TV SETS	200	5,000	4,000	4,000	7,000	20,000
VCRs	300	3,000	2,000	1,000	4,000	10,000
CAMERAS	500	200	400	400	1,000	2,000

Figure 10.4 Example of sales forecast for use in sales budget

SALES BUDGET 19×1					
PRODUCT	QUARTER				TOTAL
	1	2	3	4	
	£K	£K	£K	£K	£K
TV SETS	1,000	800	800	1,400	4,000
VCRs	900	600	300	1,200	3,000
CAMERAS	100	200	200	500	1,000
TOTALS	2,000	1,600	1,300	3,100	8,000

Figure 10.5 Example of sales budget

Because of peak sales before and after the Christmas period, the phasing of sales for this company is important to production and also with regard to cash flow.

Selling expenses budget
The selling expenses budget would include all operating expenses incurred by the sales and marketing department. These would be grouped under such headings as:

• salaries

• recruitment costs

• travel and entertaining expenses

• car costs

• advertising

• exhibitions

• literature

• free issue equipment

There could be headings such as 'new product launch expenses' and 'training costs'. In some companies the costs of postage, stationery and a portion of the cost of telephone bills and computer maintenance are also charged individually to separate departments. Each company will have its own way of deciding which costs come under administration and which costs are charged to individual departments. Figure 10.6 shows how an operating expenses budget should be prepared.

In Figure 10.6 we show the current year's budget or forecast for operating expenses as well as the budgeted increases. A figure is included for inflation, but increases (or decreases) in the budget can also result from growth or from exceptional requirements for one year. In this case a large overseas exhibition which only occurs every three years is included under the heading 'other'.

SALES DEPARTMENT OPERATING EXPENSES BUDGET FOR 19×1						
ITEM	19×0	INFLATION		GROWTH	OTHER	19×1 EXPENSES
	£K	%	£K	£K	£K	£K
Salaries	500	10	50			550
Recruitment	10	10	1			11
Travel and entertainment	80	10	8		10	98
Car costs	20	10	2	5		27
Advertising	50	10	5		10	65
Exhibitions	40	10	4		40	84
Literature	30	10	3		10	43
Sundry items	50	10	5			55
Total	780		78	5	70	933

Figure 10.6 Example of operating expenses budget

This sales expenses budget would now be included in the company total operating expenses budget and from this the profit and loss budget would be prepared.

Individual marketing plans

With a marketing plan for an individual product or market, we are not considering the total company turnover and costs, but only the additional turnover generated by the plan and the costs associated with its implementation.

There are a number of techniques that allow you to predict whether the extra business that you will generate from your plan will be profitable or not. One of the simplest is to cost up all of the expenses that you intend to incur in implementing your plan and to compare these with the contribution that will be generated by the additional sales turnover that will result from your plan.

It is necessary to cost up all of the action plans for all of the different strategies through which you intend to achieve your objectives.

Figure 10.7 shows how the figures might be prepared into a partial profit and loss account based only on *the additional costs* of implementing the marketing plan.

	19×3 £K	19×4 £K	19×5 £K
sales	400	600	750
cost of sales	240	360	450
gross profit	160	240	300
Engineering			
design and drawings	15		
testing	5		
prototypes	20		
Production			
preproduction eng	5		
Sales and Marketing			
launch package	50		
literature		5	3
advertising		5	3
exhibitions		10	5
salaries	10	5	
travel/ents	6	2	1
samples	4	2	
trial equipment	10	4	
operating expenses (relating to plan)	125	33	12
operating profit (relating to plan)	35	207	288

Figure 10.7 Effect on profit and loss account of additional operating expenses for new product introduction

In preparing this profit and loss account budget, we start at the top with the forecast sales. In the example shown, it is a new product and the sales are the sales of that product only. In the case of additional sales in a marketing plan for a new area, the additional sales forecast by the plan would be shown. The cost of sales is the direct cost, in materials and labour, of making the budgeted amount of product sold. The gross profit is the 'margin' to cover other costs and to contribute to profits.

In carrying out a marketing plan, the operating expenses incurred will relate to different departments. Most of the costs will relate to sales and marketing expenses, but if a new or modified product is involved, there will be costs involved in carrying out design work, engineering and production engineering.

In the case of the new product in Figure 10.7, there is a launch package. In the profit and loss account budget this is shown as a total figure of £50,000.

A typical launch package could include:

Promotional video £16,000
Literature £10,000
Advertising £10,000
Exhibitions £10,000
Mail Shot £4,000

These items would all be the subject of individual action plans. The action plan for the mail shot is, in fact, that shown earlier in Figure 7.4.

Other costs associated with carrying out the marketing plan would also be estimated.

The costs incurred by the sales and marketing department would represent the cost of items such as literature, advertising and exhibitions and the portion of the cost of salaries and travelling expenses that are related to this particular product. Some costs such as salaries, travel and entertainment costs are shown to be reducing after the first year of the plan. This is because these are only the partial costs of personnel directly involved in the implementation of the plan. In this case it is assumed that these personnel will only be involved in the first year to get the plan off the ground and that gradually the normal sales organization will take over. (These salary figures actually relate to part of the salary costs of a product manager managing a number of products including this one.) The costs of the normal salesforce are already included in the overall company profit and loss budget and do not therefore need to be included again in this partial profit and loss budget.

It is assumed that this is an additional product and that the sales turnover figures were not already included in the company corporate plan or in the projected profit and loss account.

Other methods used to evaluate marketing plans

The technique shown above is the most common method used by sales and marketing departments to evaluate their marketing plans. The cost of sales in Figure 10.7 is given as a fixed percentage of the sales themselves and is based upon historical data or (in the case of a new product) the best estimate available. Unless you are considering very small volumes of sales, this method is reasonably accurate, but it does assume that the cost of producing the product does not vary with the quantity produced. The cost of producing most products does in fact vary with the quantity of product produced and the technique of break-even analysis is one which takes this into account in determining the minimum volume of a product that can be profitably produced. The technique is used widely in the preparation of marketing plans – particularly in plans for new products. Before explaining what break-even analysis is and how it works, you need to understand more about different types of costs and costing techniques.

Types of costs

All costs involved in running a business can be defined as fixed, variable or semi-variable.

A **fixed cost** will remain constant even if there is a change in the level of activity of the company. This means that the fixed cost per unit of output reduces as the number of units produced increases. Marketing costs, depreciation on plant and research and development costs are all examples of fixed costs.

A **variable cost** is one which will generally vary in direct proportion to the activity of the firm, ie to the increase or decrease of production of particular products. This means that its cost per unit is the same regardless of the number of units produced. Direct material and direct labour costs are examples of variable costs.

Some costs are **step costs**, which are fixed for a certain range of activity and jump to a different level as activity increases. An example of this is the cost of sales staff where there is a step increase in cost when an additional person is recruited.

There are also **semi-variable costs** which have a fixed and a variable element. Semi-variable costs include such things as lighting, heating, power and telephones.

These types of cost can be subdivided still further. Fixed costs consist of committed costs and managed costs. Committed costs are those which cannot be eliminated or cut back without a major effect on the operation of the company and a change in its objectives – this includes costs such as management salaries and depreciation on plant or machinery. These costs can only be eliminated by getting rid of the staff concerned or by selling the machinery. Managed costs on the other hand are medium-term costs which can be increased or reduced in the short term. This would include research and development expenditure, training programmes and many of the advertising and marketing costs included in your marketing plan. Thus the costs of carrying out your action and promotion plans are mainly managed costs which can be considered in the light of the projected increase in turnover and profit that will result from them.

In your analysis of budgeted costs for your marketing plan it is usual to separate all costs into their fixed and variable elements.

Absorption costing

Absorption costing is defined as 'a method of costing in which both fixed costs and variable costs are allocated to cost units, and total overheads are absorbed according to the activity level.' With this approach to costing all costs, both fixed and variable, are apportioned to a unit of production of a particular product. An example is given in Figure 10.8.

Output in units	10,000	15,000
Variable costs	£60,000	£90,000
Fixed costs	£100,000	£100,000
Total costs	£160,000	£190,000
Cost per unit	£16	£12.67

Figure 10.8 An example of the absorption costing technique

Absorption costing has traditionally been used by accountants to value stocks and work in progress and to prepare published accounts. It is still the basis of the commonest pricing technique – cost-plus pricing, where the total cost of producing one unit of the product at the company's normal capacity level is calculated and a percentage mark-up is added. It does, however, have a number of disadvantages:

- it assumes that prices are simply a function of costs
- it does not take direct account of demand
- it is based on past costs

It can also lead to the rejection of profitable business, because the total unit cost will tend to be regarded as the lowest possible selling price. In fact, business may still be profitable at below the level of total unit cost, *if it is additional business and overheads are already covered by the normal levels of business.*

Marginal costing

Marginal costing is defined as 'the approach to costing in which only the variable costs are charged to cost units. The fixed costs are not apportioned to individual units or activities, but are met out of the total contribution generated'.

It is a more usual technique to use in the preparation of marketing plans because it allows you to carry out cost-volume-profit analysis (CVP) and to decide at what price marginal additional business is worth having.

Marginal costing deals with the relationships between five factors:

- variable costs per unit
- total fixed costs
- level of output or volume
- price of products sold
- mix of products sold

If we use the figures from Figure 10.8 and apply the marginal costing technique we get the result shown in Figure 10.9.

	Total	per unit
Sales (10,000 units)	£200,000	£20
Variable costs	£60,000	£ 6
Contribution	£140,000	
This covers the following:		
Fixed costs	£100,000	
to produce		
Net profit	£40,000	

Figure 10.9 An example of the marginal costing technique

Marginal costing allocates to products or services only those costs which vary directly with the level of activity. Fixed costs are not allocated to units of sales or production, but are treated collectively as costs for the period of time being considered.

Break-even analysis

Break-even analysis is a marginal costing technique used to evaluate the relationship between sales revenues, fixed costs and variable costs. It is widely used to evaluate the viability of new products at different levels of sales. It identifies the point at which your total revenue equals your total cost for a particular product. The break-even point determines the number of units or value of units you need to sell to cover all the costs involved in producing and selling the product. At this point the firm has no profit and no loss. Break-even analysis allows you to prepare quick estimates of how total revenue and total cost vary at different levels of expenditure for advertising, promotion and production. It enables you to make decisions on your best product mix. You can also change variables such as selling price to see how many more or less units must be sold to break even.

You need to have the following information available:

- sales price per unit

- variable costs per unit

- contribution per unit

- fixed costs per period

From this you can calculate the number of units that need to be sold to break even. You can do this by using the formula:

Sales = variable costs + fixes costs + net profit

When net profit = 0 as at the break-even point, then:

Sales = variable costs + fixed costs

If you have the following figures:

Sales price per unit   = £1,000

Variable costs per unit = £500

Contribution per unit   = £500

Fixed costs per period = £500,000

and the number of units sold = x, then:

£1,000x = £500x + £500,000

£500x = £500,000

x = 1,000

Therefore the break-even point equals 1,000 units.

This can be shown graphically as in Figure 10.10

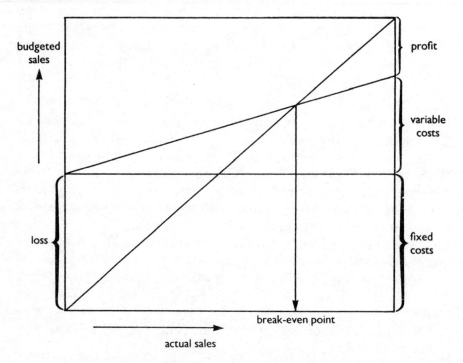

Figure 10.10 Example of break-even analysis

Any actual sales above the break-even point represent profit to the company and if sales do not reach this point a loss will be incurred.

Although you might assume that all companies need to make a profit on all products all of the time this is not necessarily so. With most products there is a market price level and if you try to sell at a price above this level you will never break into the market. This is particularly true for new consumer products where it is customary to make provision for heavy initial advertising expenditure and a forecast is made of profitability at various levels of production. It may well be the case that the product will be introduced at a loss and will only begin to contribute to the company profits after one or two years.

The break-even point can also be calculated using the principle of the contribution ratio. The contribution ratio is the contribution by the product expressed as a percentage of the sales revenue, and is particularly useful where you have a mix of more than one product line. The break-even point is expressed in the following formula:

break-even point = $\dfrac{\text{fixed costs} \times 100}{\text{contribution ratio}}$

	Product A		Product B		Total	
	£	%	£	%	£	%
Sales	100,000	100	100,000	100	200,000	100
Variable costs	40,000	40	60,000	60	100,000	50
Contribution	60,000	60	40,000	40	100,000	50
Fixed costs					80,000	40
Net profit					20,000	10

Figure 10.11 Break-even analysis for two products

In Figure 10.11 the contribution ratio is 50 per cent. The break-even point is therefore:

$\dfrac{£80,000 \times 100}{50 \text{ per cent}} = £160,000$ sales

The mix could be varied and this would change the break-even point.

Cost-volume-profit analysis and break-even analysis are concepts to be used in decision-making and will provide reasonably accurate answers. To use either technique you have to make assumptions about costs and particularly about costs being either completely fixed or completely variable throughout the range of turnover in your calculations.

Payback analysis

Another technique used with new products is payback analysis which determines the payback period, ie the time required to recover the investment made.

1. Expenditure	
Research and Development	£50,000
Production Engineering	£30,000
Tools, jigs, fixtures	£40,000
Market development	£30,000
Product launch	£20,000
Total expenditure	£170,000
2. Estimated annual contribution	
Projected sales per year	1,000
Unit contribution	£100
Total	£100,000
3. Payback in years	1.7 years

Figure 10.12 An example of payback analysis for an industrial product

To carry out payback analysis you need to determine the total money invested in the project and the estimated annual contribution to profit. Figure 10.12 shows an example of payback analysis.

Payback analysis takes no account of cash flows beyond the payback period, but it is a simple method that is particularly useful for calculating how quickly a project will pay for itself when the investment is a mixture of capital and revenue expenditure. This is common with the costing of new product launches where there will be investment in fixtures and fittings but it is not necessary for the company to invest in new machines. Costs such as production engineering, market development and product launch expenses have no residual value once they have been expended. If significant amounts of capital expenditure are necessary, other methods of capital appraisal such as the 'return on investment method' (ROI) or the 'discounted cash flow methods' (DCF) may be preferred.

Summary

Because there is no point in proceeding with your marketing plan unless it is going to increase company profits, you need to be able to evaluate its cost-effectiveness. You need to budget for the extra costs of your plan and to confirm that the return in increased contribution and profit justifies the expenditure involved.

In preparing the overall company marketing plan you must prepare the sales budget which consists of the projected sales income and the selling expenses budget. These are then fed into the overall company budget, to be included in the company business plan.

In the preparation of marketing plans for individual products or markets, you need to consider the additional turnover and contribution generated by the plan and the costs associated with its implementation. A partial profit and loss budget should be prepared.

You should use marginal costing techniques such as cost-volume-profit analysis and break-even analysis to evaluate the viability of new products at different levels of sales, and payback analysis to determine the payback period on new products.

_11_: Writing and Communicating the Marketing Plan

When you have followed through all of the stages of the marketing planning process detailed in this book, you will have collected all the information for your plan and you can then prepare the written document and ensure that you communicate it effectively to the relevant personnel in your company.

The written plan should only contain the key information that needs to be communicated – it should be clear and concise, and excessive or irrelevant detail should be excluded. The vast array of internal and external market research information collected in the course of the preparation of the plan should not be included in the written plan since it would only confuse the reader. The detail of all of the individual action plans would also be excluded from the main document. (The most important action plans, together with key market research information, may be included in appendices.)

The length of the plan will vary as, of course, a plan for a single product in a single market would be shorter than a complete marketing plan for all of a company's products in all markets.

The written document must be clear, concise and easy to read. Although the following points may seem obvious, I will state them here, as presentation of the plan to your colleagues is so important.

- Start each complete section on a new page – even if this means that some pages only have five or ten lines of text on them

- When listing key points, use double spacing

- Do not try to cram too many figures onto one page

- Do not reduce the size of documents used in the plan to a point where they become difficult to read

- Use a reasonable font size when printing the document

- If the plan is too long it will just not be read, so be ruthless and cut out unnecessary text

- Do not use any jargon that may not be understood by all those who will receive the plan, and be sure to expand any abbreviations to their full form at their first appearance

In Figure 2.2 we listed the sections of a complete marketing plan. During the rest of this chapter we will look at what information should be included in the various sections of the written plan and how it should be presented.

Table of contents

A table of contents should be included so that the various sections of the plan can be quickly and easily located. Figure 11.1 shows how the table of contents should be set out.

Section	TABLE OF CONTENTS	Page
I	INTRODUCTION	2
2	SUMMARY	3
3	SITUATION ANALYSIS – Assumptions	4
	– Sales (History/Budget)	5
	– Strategic Markets	7
	– Key Products	9
	– Key Sales Areas	11
4	MARKETING OBJECTIVES	13
5	MARKETING STRATEGIES	14
6	SCHEDULES	18
7	SALES PROMOTION	19
8	BUDGETS	20
9	PROFIT AND LOSS ACCOUNT	22
10	CONTROLS	23
11	UPDATE PROCEDURES	24
	APPENDIX 1	26
	APPENDIX 2	32

Figure 11.1 Contents list of a complete marketing plan

Introduction

This gives the background to the plan, and the reasons for its preparation, and outlines its purposes and uses. This section is an important part of individual product or market plans. In the case of the annual company marketing plan, it would be expanded to include reference to the key factors that have affected business over the previous twelve months.

For a company selling, for example, a product to the water industry, the introduction to their plan might be:

'The company has always sold a small amount of product into the UK water industry, but it has never been a key activity area. Because of this, we knew little of the industry or of the potential in it for our product. With the privatization of the water industry and the announcement by the water minister that the industry is budgeting for a capital improvement programme of £17.3 billion, it was felt by the sales and marketing director that we needed to analyse our position in this market and to prepare for growth to take advantage of the increased level of spending by the industry.'

Summary

The summary should present the key points of the plan in a clear and concise form. All personnel receiving the plan should be able to understand the essence of the plan from this summary.

The summary should always include:

• The underlying assumptions on which the plan is based

• The objectives of the plan

• The time-scale over which the plan will be implemented

For an existing product, the summary of the plan could be:

'Sales of the product in the UK market have increased by 30 per cent in real terms in the last 3 years. We still only have a 5 per cent share of the total market and we believe that if economic conditions remain stable, we will be able to continue to gain market share in an expanding market. The objective of this plan is to achieve a further 30 per cent growth in real terms over the next 3 years, giving the company a 6 per cent share of the projected market in 19X1. The plan details how this can be achieved profitably and without any major additional investment in plant and machinery.'

For a new product, the format of the summary could be as follows:

'Based on our analysis of the market and our estimate of the costs and likely selling price of the new product, this plan shows how the product could achieve sales of £1 million per year within three years and the contribution would be such that the payback period would be less than two years.'

Situation analysis

In the written plan, the situation analysis should include only the summaries of the external and internal marketing research and the resulting SWOT analysis. These are included under the headings:

- The assumptions
- A summary of historical and budgeted sales
- A review of strategic markets
- A review of key products
- A review of key sales areas

There will be some overlap between the reviews of strategic markets, key products and key sales areas, because it is possible to show the mix in different ways. Key products can be shown by market and sales area and key markets can be shown by product and sales area. The important thing is to present the information in a manner that highlights the key points you are trying to convey to those who read the plan.

Assumptions

These are the key facts and assumptions on which the plan is based. They should be few in number and should relate only to the key issues which would significantly affect the likelihood of the plan's marketing objectives being achieved.

Each assumption should be a brief factual statement. For example:

- The £/$ exchange rate will remain in the range $1.40 to $1.70 :£1 for the next 12 months
- Interest rates will start to reduce from present levels by the end of the year
- Water privatization will go ahead this year
- The present import restraint level of 10 per cent of the market share is respected by the Japanese

202 • THE MARKETING PLAN

Sales

In this section of your marketing plan, historical sales going back three years should be included together with sales forecasts for the next three years. More detail would normally be included with regard to the next twelve months' sales forecast since this will become the annual budget for the product or area covered by the plan. The forecasts for subsequent years assume that the first year's figures will be achieved and may be revised in the light of actual results when the plan itself is revised in subsequent years. Since the profitability of these sales is paramount, details of the margins and profitability of the product should also be included in this section. The format for setting out this information should follow the guidelines given in Chapter 4.

It is important to indicate whether the years shown in the forecast are calendar years or financial years beginning on a date other than 1 January – many companies, of course, use 1 April. You should also make it clear which years' figures are actual figures for sales and which are forecasts. Although this will be clear to you when you write the plan, in two or three years' time the dates of the forecast years will have become actual dates and there could be confusion.

You should use invoiced sales rather than order intake figures as the basis of the plan, because other departments in the company, such as production and finance, can only operate on sales figures. You will, however, need to include order intake figures as well, because these will be the order budgets that the sales department will work to. You should state whether the figures are based on current year prices or whether they have been inflation adjusted – if they have been then the figure that you have assumed for inflation should be included.

Sales Figures (Historical and Forecast)					
(All values in £K at actual)					
				◄——— projected ———►	
Year	19x0	19x1	19x2	19x3	19x4	19x5
UK	100	60	100	80	100	100
Europe	318	320	322	320	320	340
Other	40	80	80	120	130	140
Total	458	460	502	520	550	580

Figure 11.2 Format for sales projection

Figure 11.2 shows a typical set of sales figures.

Other examples were shown in Chapter 6 in Figures 6.11, 6.12 and 6.13.

Strategic markets

In this section you should include historical information and forecasts for the company's sales in key industry sectors. The information can be presented in two ways:

- Showing the percentage of company sales into each market

- Showing the percentage share of individual industrial markets that the company believes that it has

Only include your key markets – ideally this should be between three and six industries, because if you only sell to one industry you will be very vulnerable to changes or fluctuations within that industry.

This type of information can either be presented in tabular form as in Figures 11.3 and 11.4 or in graphical form as in Figure 11.5.

Product: Valves	Actual – 19×1		Forecast – 19×4	
Industry	£K	%	£K	%
Water	2,220	28.1	3,600	36.7
Chem/Petrochem	1,600	20.3	1,700	17.4
Paper	850	10.8	1,000	10.2
Food	620	7.9	700	7.1
Other	2,600	32.9	2,800	28.6
Total	7,890	100.0	9,800	100.0

Figure 11.3 Presentation of sales by strategic market

COMPANY STRATEGIC MARKETS						
Area: UK	Product: Centrifuges					
	19×0		19×1		19×2	
	Sales	Market share	Sales	Market share	Sales	Market share
Industry	£K	%	£K	%	£K	%
Sugar	200	40	250	40	300	40
Chemicals	228	14	280	17	400	19
Sewage	108	23	150	24	210	25

Figure 11.4 Presentation of sales and market share by strategic market

As well as figures, it is important that the plan should include narrative relating to each of the strategic markets. This should

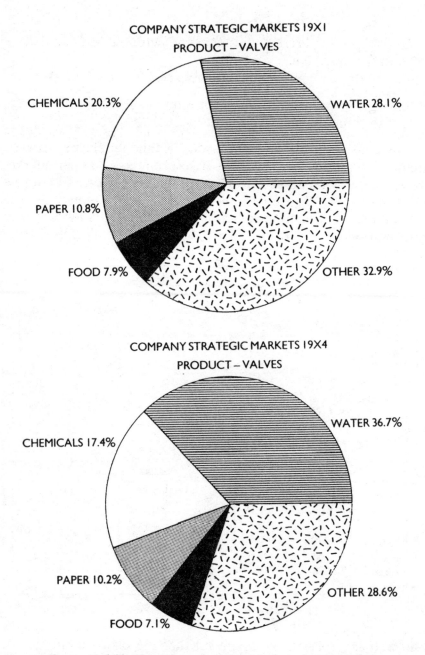

Figure 11.5 Graphical/representation of strategic markets

include details of whether the market is increasing or decreasing and whether your share of the market is increasing or decreasing. Key segments within markets should also be highlighted. You may have identified the food industry as a strategic market, but your business is unlikely to be spread equally across the whole of that industry. It may be that most of your sales to the food industry go to biscuit manufacturers or butter manufacturers. This should be stated in the narrative.

Key products

This section lists your key products and details technological and commercial factors relating to them. This would include the results of the SWOT analysis on your products and your competitor's products. It would also include information on sales and market shares for individual products. This could be presented using a similar format to Figure 11.4, or it could be presented for the product portfolio using the Boston Matrix approach as shown in Figure 11.6.

PRODUCT PORTFOLIO GROWTH 19X1–19X3

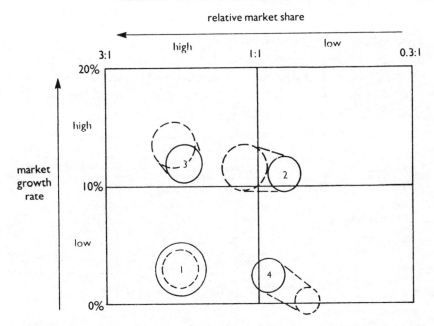

1 = bath taps
2 = mixer taps
3 = shower attachments
3 = brass taps

Figure 11.6 Presentation of product portfolio matrix

For a company manufacturing fruit jams, marmalades and fruit pie fillers, a key product would be whole-fruit jams. The strengths and weaknesses of this product would be presented as shown in Figure 11.7.

KEY PRODUCT	WHOLE FRUIT JAM
STRENGTHS	WEAKNESSES
Use whole fruit	Premium priced
High fruit content	Limited range of flavours
Clear colour	Low volume production
Seen as quality product	Use artificial colours
Good brand name	Use artificial preservatives
OPPORTUNITIES	THREATS
Develop wider range	Competitors have a wider range of flavours
Develop natural range without artificial colours/preservatives	Competitors avoid artificial colours
	Low priced imports

Figure 11.7 Presentation of key product information for a jam manufacturer

Key sales areas

This information would be presented in the same way as the information on strategic markets, but it would give the information relating to geographical sales areas instead of industry sectors. The information can be presented in tabular form as in Figure 11.8 or in graphical form as in Figure 11.9.

KEY SALES AREAS				
Product: Valves	Actual – 19×1		Forecast – 19×4	
Area	£K	%	£K	%
UK	4,460	56.5	5,520	56.3
Other Europe	1,107	14.0	1,215	12.4
USA	1,403	17.8	2,042	20.8
Rest of World	920	11.7	1,023	10.5
Total	7,890	100.0	9,800	100.0

Figure 11.8 Representation of key sales areas

In the narrative you should include information on the size of each key market, growth rates, and your position in each market now and projected for the future. You should also include comments which may relate to your distributor, agent or other methods of distribution in that market.

Marketing objectives

This is a list of objectives that are to be achieved, quantified in terms of order intake, sales turnover, market share and profit. In the written plan you should list your key objectives only. The key objectives are the overall objectives. A key objective could be:

'To increase order intake by 5 per cent per year in real terms for the next 3 years.'

Other objectives that contribute to this key objective could be:

'To increase order intake in the UK by 10 per cent per year in real terms for the next 3 years. To retain current order intake levels in the rest of Europe over the next 3 years. To increase order intake in the USA by 3 per cent per year in real terms for the next 3 years.'

If the order intake figures are already included in the plan together with the sales figures, the same objective could be simply written as:

'To increase order intake/invoiced sales by the amounts shown in section 3.2 of the plan.'

Marketing strategies

You should indicate whether you are adopting defensive, developing, or attacking strategies – or a mixture of different types. The individual strategies should then be listed under the headings of the four main elements of the marketing mix:

• Strategies relating to products

• Strategies relating to pricing

• Strategies relating to advertising/promotion

• Strategies relating to distribution

There may be some overlap between the individual categories, but this does not matter so long as all of the strategies are

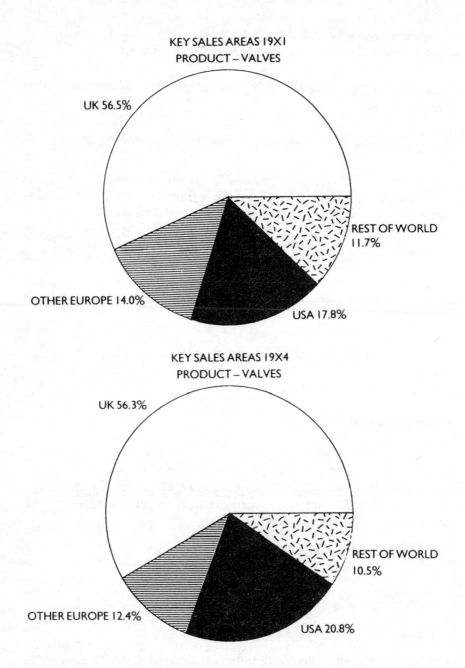

KEY SALES AREAS 19X1
PRODUCT – VALVES

UK 56.5%

REST OF WORLD
11.7%

OTHER EUROPE 14.0%

USA 17.8%

KEY SALES AREAS 19X4
PRODUCT – VALVES

UK 56.3%

REST OF WORLD
10.5%

OTHER EUROPE 12.4%

USA 20.8%

Figure 11.9 Graphical representation of key sales areas

listed. A pricing strategy for a product could be included under both 'products' and 'pricing'. A change in the organization of the salesforce for a product could be included under the headings 'products' and 'promotion'. Another way of listing the strategies is to put together a separate list of strategies for each individual product that is included in the plan. An example of this is given in Figure 11.10.

Product: Ball valve
Objective: To increase share of US market from 1% to 4% within 3 years

Strategies:
Product   –   Redesign unit for US market and incorporate inch sizes and ASA flange options
Pricing   –   Keep price increases to 2% below the US inflation rate for next 3 years
Promotion   –   Hold regional training courses in USA
                –   Implement major advertising campaign
                –   Exhibit at key exhibitions in USA
Distribution –   Set up new sales network with regional and industry sales managers

Figure 11.10 Strategies for an individual product

Schedule of what/where/how

This is the master schedule showing the programme for the implementation of the action plans. Each action plan would be listed either in the master schedule or in a sub-schedule for the functions of product, pricing, promotion or distribution. These schedules indicate to each department and to each member of staff their responsibilities and the timetable for carrying them out. They should take the form of bar charts. An example is given in Figure 11.11.

The detailed individual action plans would not be included in the main body of the marketing plan. They would either be included as an appendix to the main plan or would be communicated separately to those who are to carry them out.

Sales promotion

Under this heading you should detail your advertising and promotions plan. This includes your personnel requirements as well as advertising and sales promotion.

MASTER SCHEDULE		
Product: Ball Valves		
Area: USA		
Year: 19×1		

Month	1 2 3 4 5 6 7 8 9 10 11 12	Responsibility	
Action Plan		Dept	Person
Redesign	————x	Eng	ILT
Pricing	————x	Sales	AJK
Training	——————x	Serv	EGT
Advertising	——————x	Sales	AJK
Exhibitions	——————x	Sales	AJK
Distribution	—————x	Sales	AJK

Figure 11.11 Master schedule for a plan for a product in the USA

You should define the mix of distribution channels that you will be using and the structure of your sales organization, including any changes that you intend to make as part of your plan. You should include a list of existing and additional sales personnel as well as an organization chart for the sales department. Examples of sales organization charts and the presentation of existing and additional personnel were given in Chapter 8 (Figures 8.7 and 8.8 and Table 8.1).

You should include the details and costs of your advertising and sales promotion campaigns including an advertising and promotions schedule for the next twelve months.

Budgets

The minimum information that should be included in this section is the total cost of implementing the plan. This needs to confirm that the return in increased contribution and profit justifies the expenditure in the action plans and the advertising and promotion plan. In many sales organizations, the calculations with regard to contribution and profit are carried out separately by the accounting and finance function of the company. It is therefore common, in this section of the written plan, just to include the costs of implementing the plan and to pass the marketing plan forward to be included in the preparation of the written corporate or business plan of the company. The disadvantage of this approach is that it removes the necessity from the sales and marketing organization of being able fully to justify the costs of the implementation of their plan.

If the plan is for a new product or new market, this section would include the extra costs of the plan over and above the normal sales and marketing budget. With a new product there should always be a financial justification of the product.

Profit and loss account

The budgeted extra sales and budgeted extra costs will have an effect on the company profit and loss account. The additional sales projected by the plan and the extra costs involved must be presented in the written plan in a way that shows the extra contribution that the plan will make to company profits. The figures should be presented as shown in Figure 10.7.

Controls

It is important to have a suitable monitoring and control system to measure performance in achieving the objectives of the marketing plan and to recommend corrective action where necessary. This monitoring and control system should be included in the written plan.

The control process involves:

• Establishing standards – these would relate to the budgeted sales and costs and the time-scales for the implementation of the action plans.

• Measuring performance – this would compare actual performance against the standards.

• Proposing measures to correct deviations from the standard – by detailing corrective procedures to be implemented if the variation from standard exceeds certain limits. These limits should be defined in the written plan.

The control system will operate on the people who are responsible for implementing the plan rather than the schedules and costs themselves. The control system should be easy to operate and should allow reasonable variations from the standards before it comes into action. When changes from standard are detected you should investigate and determine the cause before taking corrective action.

The controls should be detailed in the written plan. They could include:

'A summary of costs against budget and actual progress against schedules to be prepared every three months'

'A report on the implementation of the action plans to be presented at the quarterly marketing planning meetings'

Update procedures

In preparing your marketing plan you will have set up a marketing planning system and have carried out marketing planning in a structured way. Once set up, this marketing planning system can be used in the future.

Similarly your marketing plan is not set in stone. As you implement it you will find that economic conditions may change, certain strategies may not be as effective as you thought and there may be delays in the implementation of some of the action plans. It may not prove to be as easy as expected to recruit certain additional personnel and others may leave the company. Conversely the plan may prove more successful than you anticipated and order intake levels expected in two years may be achieved in one year.

The implementation of your marketing plan should be monitored and if major deviations occur, you may need to modify objectives, change strategies, or revise schedules and budgets. An update procedure should be included in the written plan. This may simply state 'This plan is to be revised every 12 months'. Certainly, all plans should be updated on an annual basis. This holds for an individual plan for an individual product or market just as well as for a complete marketing plan for all products in all markets.

Communicating the plan

Your task is not over when the written plan is complete. It must then be communicated to those who will implement it. If a plan is not properly communicated, it will fail. You do not want the plan just to sit on a shelf unused because it was not understood. So it is important to present the plan and to make sure that everyone understands it, rather than just sending a written copy in the internal mail. Remember that the contributors to the plan will be better motivated to help implement it if they have been involved in the planning process.

It can be a mistake to distribute the complete plan too widely – the UK sales manager does not need all of the detail of the export plan and likewise the export sales manager does not need all that of the UK plan. Also, the complete plan is a sensitive and confidential document that would be of considerable interest to competitors and could be damaging to the company in the wrong hands. Personnel do move on and they take information with them. Distribution of the complete plan should be as a controlled, numbered document.

If you split the master marketing plan up into sub-plans, the various parts of it can then be easily distributed to the relevant company personnel. Each manager would then pass the appropriate sections of the plan to those in his department as required. You should have meetings to explain to the various managers and salesmen how the provisions of the plan will affect them, to ensure that everyone understands the plan and how it is to be implemented. This would also provide the opportunity for feedback from all levels within the organization.

Copies would obviously be supplied to the senior executives of the company, but the plan should also be distributed to the heads of departments such as accounts, R & D and manufacturing who would be affected by or involved in its implementation.

Summary

The written plan is the document that will transmit the detail of the plan to those who will implement it. It should only contain the key information that needs to be communicated. Excessive and irrelevant detail should be excluded.

The information should be presented in a logical order. It should include an introduction giving the background to the plan, the reasons for its preparation and its purposes and uses, and also a summary which should present the key points of the plan in clear and concise form.

The assumptions on which the plan is based should be clearly stated and information on sales, strategic markets, key products and key sales areas should be presented.

The marketing objectives are the aims of the plan and the strategies explain how these objectives will be achieved. The master schedule is the programme for the implementation of the action plans.

The advertising and promotions plan includes personnel requirements as well as advertising and sales promotion. The total cost of implementing the plan and its justification must be shown.

The plan needs to have a suitable control system to measure performance in achieving its objectives and to recommend corrective action where necessary. The plan needs to be properly communicated to those who will be implementing it. It needs to be presented rather than just arriving in the internal mail.

Conclusion

In preparing your marketing plan you will have set up a marketing planning system and carried out marketing planning in a structured way. This marketing planning system can be kept in place and used in the future.

If you involve others in the preparation of the plan it becomes 'everyone's plan' rather than just 'your plan' and it will be implemented more fervently. The team that has just worked through the planning process will have learnt a lot about the company and its products. They will have a better understanding of the marketplace and how the company and the products fit into it.

The experience that they have gained will make your company's marketing planning easier and more professional in future years. Practice makes better, but not perfect, and each time the marketing planning process is followed through, the results will improve.

With the best planning in the world, markets are still affected by forces outside your control, but with a proper marketing plan and an understanding of the marketing planning process you can adapt to the changing conditions of the competitive world in which we live.

Useful Addresses

Government statistics (UK and other)

Government Statistics – A Brief Guide to Sources

Available free from:

Information Services Division,
Central Statisical Office,
Great George Street,
London SW1P 3AQ
Tel: 0171-270 6363/4

Guide to Official Statistics

Available from:

HMSO Publications Centre,
PO Box 276,
London SW8 5DR.
Tel: 0171-873 0011

Statistical information can be consulted at:

Central Statistical Office Library,
Government Buildings,
Cardiff Road,
Newport, Gwent NP9 1XG.
Tel: 01633 812973
(UK Manufacturing and Production Statistics)

The DTI Export Market Information Centre (EMIC),
Kingsgate House,
66–74 Victoria Street,
London SW1E 6SW.
Tel: 0171-215 5444/5
(Import/Export Information for the whole world plus Trade Directories)

Other general sources

Market Research GB
Market Research Europe
Market Research International
Retail Monitor International

Over 100 Directories, Handbooks and Statistical Sourcebooks

Available from:

Euromonitor
60–61 Britton Street,
London EC1M 5NA.
Tel: 0171-251 8024

The Source Book

Available from:

Key Note Publications Ltd,
Field House,
72 Oldfield Road,
Hampton,
Middlesex TW12 2HQ.
Tel: 0181-783 0755

Directories

Kompass Directories (UK and 20 foreign country directories)

Kelly's Business Directory
Dial Industry

Available from:

Reed Information Services,
Windsor Court,
East Grinstead House,
East Grinstead,
West Sussex RH19 1XA.
Tel: 01342-335928

Financial data

The Companies Registration Office,
Companies House,
55–71 City Road,
London EC1Y 1AY.
Tel: 0171-253 9393

Dun and Bradstreet,
Holmers Farm Way,
High Wycombe,
Bucks HP12 4UL.
Tel: 01494-422299

Business ratio reports

ICC Business Publications,
Field House,
72 Oldfield Road,
Hampton,
Middlesex TW12 2HQ.
Tel: 0181-783 0922

Market reports

Key Note Publications Ltd,
Field House,
72 Oldfield Road
Hampton,
Middlesex TW12 2HQ.
Tel: 0181-783 0755

Euromonitor,
60–61 Britton Street,
London EC1M 5NA.
Tel: 0171-251 8024

Mintel International Group Ltd,
18/19 Long Lane,
London EC1A 9HE.
Tel: 0171-606 4533

Frost and Sullivan Inc,
Sullivan House,
4 Grosvenor Gardens,
London SW1W 0DH.
Tel: 0171-730 3438

Market research organizations

The Market Research Society Yearbook

Available from:

The Market Research Society,
15 Northburgh Street,
London EC1V 0AH.
Tel: 0171-490 4911

The Association of Market Survey Organizations (AMSO),
16 Creighton Avenue,
London N10 1NU.
Tel: 0181-444 3692

CACI Market Analysis Ltd,
CACI House,
Kensington Village,
Avonmore Road,
London W14 8TH.
Tel: 0171-602 6000

The Chartered Institute of Marketing,
Moor Hall,
Cookham,
Maidenhead,
Berkshire SL6 9QH.
Tel: 01628-524922

Trade associations

Directory of British Associations

CBD Research Ltd,
Chancery House,
15 Wickham Road,
Beckenham,
Kent BR3 2JS.
Tel: 0181-650 7745

Bibliography

Ansoff, I (1975), *Corporate Planning*, Penguin Books, London.

Bland, M (1981), *Be Your Own PR Man*, Kogan Page, London.

Courtis, J (1987), *Marketing Services*, Kogan Page, London.

Dudley, J (1989), *1992 – Strategies for the Single Market*, Kogan Page, London.

Gabor, A (1977) *Pricing: Principles and Practices*, Heinemann Educational, London.

Giles, G B (1966), *Marketing Management*, M&E Handbook, Pitman Publishing, London.

Harrison, J. (1989), *Finance for the Non-Financial Manager*, Guild Publishing, London.

Kidron, M and Segal, R (1984), The New State of the World Atlas, Pan Books, London.

Small, J (1986), *Business Ratios*, ICC Business Ratios, London.

Spillard, P 2nd Edn (1975), *Sales Promotion – Its Place in Marketing Strategy*, Business Books, London.

St John Bate, J (1987), Business Computing with the Amstrad PC 1640, BSP Professional Books, Oxford.

Standard Industrial Classification of Economic Activities 1992, Her Majesty's Stationery Office (HMSO), London.

Standard International Trade Classification, (Revision 3), Series M, No. 34/Rev.3, United Nations Publications.

Warren, R (1988), *How to Understand and Use Company Accounts*, Hutchinson Books, London.

Index